M000004389

The Stories We Neglect to Share

AN ANTHOLOGY

The events and conversations in this book have been set down to the best of the authors' ability, although some names and details have been changed to protect the privacy of individuals.

Copyright © 2020 by Trust Tree Productions

All rights reserved. No part of this book may be reproduced or used in any manner without written permission of the copyright owner except for the use of quotations in a book review.
For more information, address: contact@trusttreegroup.com

First edition September 2020

Book design by Brenda Rose
www.brendarose.com

ISBN 978-0-578-75181-8
www.trusttreegroup.com

Dedicated to Mary Granger and Nan Hendrickson
and to the women who inspired us to share extraordinary stories

Acknowledgements

"There is no greater agony than bearing an untold story inside of you."
– Dr. Maya Angelou

We are not meant to do important things alone; we are meant to do them together. There are so many wonderful people who assisted us with the concept and execution of this book. Without them, there would be no book. Here are some of them:

Brenda Rose – deepest thanks to Brenda who took our concept and brought it to life through her exceptional design skills and also we appreciate you holding our hands through the publishing process.

Betty Sue Morris, for being the first one to say yes.

Thanks to all the women who provided their stories, we are forever in awe of your courage and we hope we've done you justice

Thanks to our Trust Tree Tribe who inspire us and delight us every day, virtually and IRL – we see you and look forward to continuing with you on the path of honoring our stories and holding space for each other.

Big shout out to Chris, who is not only our podcast producer but our Yoda when we need it.

To our husbands for infinite patience and wise counsel.

To our families for support and cheerleading beyond what we ever imagined. Special thank you to our sisters who allowed us to include their words in this book. Your generosity is immense.

We started this project in the world before COVID and brought it to life in the midst of a pandemic, economic collapse, racial reckoning and political unrest unlike any we've seen in our lifetimes. Along the way we became more convinced than ever of the primary importance of women's stories and perspectives in how we evolve and move forward in healing our society. We hope these stories moved you as they have changed us.

Thank you for the privilege of providing a platform for these incredible women.

Contents

Introduction

"If we want to change the stories being told, we have to change the storytellers." – Reese Witherspoon

The idea that we would publish an anthology of women's stories came from reading the above Reese Witherspoon quote and taking it to heart. We created Trust Tree out of our desire to find new ways for women to connect and support each other through the ups and downs of life. Lots of our early conversations centered on how great it would have been if we'd been able to hear the stories of struggles of others instead of the sanitized versions we are often given of "it was really hard and then everything was great".

We knew there were deeply textured stories out there that reflected the richness and complexities of women's lives and saw that there weren't enough places telling the stories of the extraordinary lives of seemingly ordinary women. We say seemingly ordinary because we don't believe there are any ordinary lives as defined by our modern culture. Perhaps not all of these women are living high profile lives but that doesn't mean their contributions shouldn't be honored and celebrated. Ordinary people change the world every day.

Originally, our goal was to produce a short film about the life of one of the community treasures of Camas, Washington, former mayor Nan Hendricksen. We'd both known Nan for years in the way you do when your circles overlap but not too deeply. Nan participated in a panel discussion and dug deeper into the genesis of her calling to public service. Nan was willing to share the reality of her challenges in the role. She was delightfully forthcoming about the very real pain points involved in being a single mother with a full time job in addition to leading a city. A city that was in the throes of navigating a new economic course as the natural resource economy they had relied on bottomed out. It was a an era of transformation and Nan was at the helm. Incredibly difficult and yet, there was Nan. She'd suffered and persevered and here she was, an example we could all learn from.

We couldn't help wondering, why hadn't we heard this kind of detail of Nan's story before? And, oh man, we wanted to share it with everyone!

We plunged into figuring out what's involved in producing a movie and got a quick education in the challenges associated with raising funds for a film project. In the meantime we got to thinking about all the other women we know and how we only knew a piece of their stories. What kind of gems would we find if we dug deeper? And as the realities of producing even a short film presented themselves, we were quickly learning that collecting women's stories and getting them out in the world was going to require multiple platforms. We were impatient to gather women's stories and share them. How could we find women who were willing to go on this ride with us?

Enter Purpose Dinners. Yes, we started by gathering different groups of women together for Purpose Dinners. Our intent behind these dinners was to create a space to share stories by telling our own and asking the women around the table to talk about their lives. Their high points, their lessons, their loves. Those were powerful evenings that formed bonds between women who might have never met each other. We were blown away by the response but knew we wanted to share those stories with an even wider audience.

When we hit on the idea of an anthology it felt like the next logical step. Nevermind that neither of us had ever published a book before. A little detail like that had never stopped us before. The next question was what would we center the stories around?

Enter our local wonder woman, the late Mary Granger. Mary was a Vancouver, Washington resident who led many charitable efforts in our community, including founding our local Community Foundation and sponsoring an I Have a Dream program for an underserved elementary school. In doing the research about Mary to feature her and all her good works during Women's History Month in 2019 we ran across her obituary and that got us to wondering about all the stories that don't get told in our obituaries. Whether from lack of space or because they are stories no one knows about us, what are the stories that don't make it into our obituaries? And what do we want known about us when we die?

As we sat down with several of the women we were hoping would contribute, we were met with a variety of responses, almost all of them involved a strong emotional component. These amazing, accomplished women were often overcome with emotion at being asked to share their stories. We committed to working our way through learning how do publish an anthology in part to honor this heartfelt response. It means something when someone sees you and wants to hear your story.

We hope this is the first of many books profiling extraordinary women: their stories, their trials, their tribe and their triumphs.

It is thrilling that you now have this book in your hands. The stories reflect the unique strength, resilience and humor of women. This book is intended to be a celebration of all the stories that get told and those that didn't have an opportunity to be told.

We see you.

"From a young age death has always been something that is talked about, isn't feared and is a normal part of life."

Family Plots

- Lindsay Fisher

I was 11 years old when the coming of age movie *My Girl* was released. I instantly felt a connection with the main character, young Veda Sultenfuss. Much to my delight, Veda lived with her funeral director father who ran the town funeral home out of their home. I, too, had a father and a grandfather who were funeral directors and owned and operated our family business, Evergreen Memorial Gardens Cemetery, Funeral Chapel and Crematory. While I didn't live at the funeral home, I grew up in and around the profession. As my peers all began to watch the movie they started to express curiosity about what my family did for a living. It was the first time that I realized just how unique my family's profession was.

Through my younger years I helped visitors during Memorial Day Weekend and during my teenage years I began working in our Cemetery Office. My mother would often give my sister and I the location of a burial in the cemetery to place a flag or flowers. Like a morbid scavenger hunt, off we would go with a map and coordinates in hand into the 40-acre cemetery. We would return, excited to report back that we had been successful with our assigned task. What was framed as a fun game was actually a sneak peek into our business' paramount responsibility of honoring lives lived.

At one point, while I was in high school, I actually got fired by my dad. Time has softened the story behind my firing. I was probably late for curfew or, in true teenagefashion, talked back. The reason was not work related; however, when working for a family business those lines often get blurred. Things calmed down and I showed back up to work the following day. The firing was never talked about again.

There was a rule that after college I had to gain other professional experience outside of the family business. After spending some time in the hotel industry gaining management experience in a corporate environment, I felt a call to come home. I wanted the opportunity to carry on the family legacy of being funeral directors and learn from my father; to continue what my grandparents had started back in 1968 through sacrifice and hard work. On my last day in the hotel, the General Manager pointed out some similarities in the two professions. He joked that now "my guests would check in, but they just won't check out!"

I bravely sent my dad a resume and cover letter and awaited a response. Once my dad received my resume, I got a phone call asking to speak with "Mrs. Fisher" to schedule an interview. Our intense two hour interview was very nontraditional in nature, but he had valid concerns about introducing the third generation to the family business. There were questions like, "will you and your sister be able to get along at work?" and "how will you handle being the boss's child?" The positives I brought to the operation were greater than his reservations and, in the end, I got the job!

Being the boss's child, and even more importantly, the boss's daughter, has been more challenging than I ever expected. From the outside, it was easy to assume that I was just handed the position. Unaware of the professional experience and knowledge I was bringing from my career in hospitality back to the family business, some people resented me. I jumped in managing employees that my father, and in some cases, my grandfather had hired. On the day that I started, there were members of the team that had worked at Evergreen Memorial Gardens longer than I had been alive. Understandably, it was hard for someone who remembered me in diapers to now see me in a new managerial role. I had always been the 'boss's kid' and now they had to take me seriously and take direction from me.

There have been many instances in which I would give an answer to an employee's question or make a decision regarding how to handle a situation that was unpopular. Hoping to get a different answer or just not wanting to listen to me, the employee would turn around and ask my dad the same question. Thankfully my dad, my boss, would back my decision in the presence of the employee, but in private he would tell me how he would do things differently next time. By doing this he provided a learning opportunity for the employee and a chance to help develop me as a manager.

Women in the death care profession and in leadership face gender stereotypes. There are assumptions made about our ability to lift or handle the physical rigors of the job. I have received phone calls from people asking to speak with the manager, but stated they only wanted to speak with a man. With a smile, I answered their call and greeted them by saying, "my name is Lindsay and I am the manager. I am sorry to disappoint you, but I am indeed a female and I am happy to help you." Just another not so subtle reminder that our society still has more ground to cover to achieve workplace equality.

Death isn't a 9-5 job. It doesn't care that it is a holiday or the middle of the night. It took me proving that I was willing to work the long hours, the evenings and the holidays to gain the respect of those that report to me. There was no job or task that I wasn't willing to do. I wasn't afraid to put on my boots to work on the cemetery grounds and get my hands dirty. Through my actions, I showed that I earned my position. Not because it was a birthright or because I was given preferential treatment. I don't view the challenges I faced as being a test, but instead they were an opportunity for me to prove who I really was.

My wonderful husband, PJ, and I decided to start a family of our own. When each boy was in their first few weeks of life I returned to work with them in tow. It felt natural because that is where our whole family spent their days together. It is our home away from home. Growing up in a cemetery, funeral chapel and crematory exposed them to unique situations. Other children had typical early words like, cat and dog. Our children's early language development included words such as urn and casket. People were delighted to see young children when they walked into an uncomfortable place like the cemetery office or funeral home. Having the boys greet people when they arrived on a difficult day softened the environment and made it less scary.

In Kindergarten, our oldest son had a classmate's mother die unexpectedly from an aneurysm. It was hard for the young students to fathom the loss of a parent. Jack came home with many questions and wanted to know if his friend's mother was at our funeral home. I confirmed that she indeed was. Jack returned to school the next day informing all of his friends in an attempt to comfort them that "it was ok because my mommy is taking care of his mommy." From a young age death has always been something that is talked about, isn't feared and is a normal part of life. As a society, we have a long way to go in embracing death. My family and I are ambassadors to encourage difficult conversations about death and end of life decisions.

People often ask, "isn't your job difficult?" or, "isn't it sad all of the time?" Yes, it can be difficult and every day is filled with sad stories. I get calls from family friends and many times the only words they can muster are, "Lindsay, we need your help." The heaviness of each day is made lighter knowing that I can help when most people don't know what to do. I am honored to be the person that they call at the worst time of their lives.

In April 2015 my personal life and professional life collided. Our family returned from a wonderful family vacation in San Diego and I had caught a cold from our youngest. I discovered a swollen lymph node near my collarbone, but I dismissed it as a side effect of being sick. The swelling wasn't visible to others and could barely be felt. My husband encouraged me to call my doctor anyway to be sure it was nothing. Upon arriving at the doctor's office and describing my symptoms she was instantly concerned. Over the next 10 days, after a whirlwind of tests, doctor appointments and surgery, I received the phone call that I had been diagnosed with Hodgkin's Lymphoma. At 35 years old, I was facing my own mortality.

Looking our two boys, ages 4 and 7, in the face and telling them that *Mommy has cancer* was the most difficult thing that I have ever had to do. My husband gave me 24 hours to feel sorry for myself and then we were coming up with a plan and fighting. Cruel and insensitive? No, just the opposite. He knew that if I continued to feel sorry for myself, there I would stay. Instead I knew that I had a partner to stand shoulder to shoulder with me. While part of the fighting included chemo and treatments, part of my planning included making sure my final wishes were written down. I had spent my career preaching to others about the importance of making pre-arrangements and making sure people's loved ones knew what their wishes were. Now, it was my turn to go through the same exercise; to practice what I preach.

Thankfully my written wishes can remain on the shelf until they are needed because I have remained in remission after my last chemo. My life experiences and receiving a cancer diagnosis have made me better at my job. I can often relate more to the families that I serve through a similar shared experience. I pray when the day comes that my written wishes are needed, my legacy is that my life's work is an outward expression of what is in my heart and a reflection of my faith. It is my calling to care for the broken hearted, befriend the lonely and help the helpless.

Lindsay Fisher, Vice President of Administration has been with Evergreen Memorial Gardens Cemetery, Funeral Chapel and Crematory since February 2006. She attended LaSalle High School in Milwaukie, Oregon. In 2003 she graduated from Washington State University with a degree in Hospitality Business Management and a second degree in Business Management. She has been a licensed Funeral Director since August 2012.

Lindsay is a member of the 2015 class of Leadership Clark County and received the Vancouver Business Journal's Accomplished and Under 40 honor that same year. She has received the Paul Harris award from the Rotary Club of Greater Clark County. She serves on the board of the Association of Washington Business and the Trauma Intervention Program Advisory Council. She was appointed to Washington State University Vancouver Chancellor's Advisory Council in 2015 and now serves as the Council Chair since 2018.

Lindsay enjoys traveling, concerts and spending time with her friends and family. She is involved in many community service activities and various boards and committees. Lindsay has been married to her husband, P.J., since 2005 and together they have two sons.

"But funny thing
about luck.
It changes.
Almost inevitably."

Modern Lover

- Beth Harrington

Obituaries state the facts of one's life, but too often don't fully represent what those facts meant to the deceased. The "Irish Sports Page" (my grandmother taught me that one) with its dates and locales and affiliations and next of kin didn't always communicate the catalyzing forces in a person's trajectory.

So when asked to imagine my obituary, I'm guessing it will note my career as an independent filmmaker. And maybe it will glancingly mention my time as a member of a quirky, culty rock band. But the bigger emphasis will be given to the time I spent making movies.

Which is funny because the lessons I learned that made it possible for me to really make films came from my earliest days in rock and roll.

In my mid-20s, years before I had a chance to dig deeply into being a filmmaker (which had sorta been the point of my college education in communications - ahem), I veered radically off the road and became a member of Jonathan Richman and The Modern Lovers. The Modern Lovers was a long-standing musical "institution" with an ever-changing lineup (originating in Boston in the late '60s and continuing into the mid-'80s). For those who can remember the '80s, it might be edifying to know that future members of The Cars, Talking Heads, and The Real Kids emerged from the Modern Lovers' ranks. Though the personnel changed, one constant was the band's leader, the singer, songwriter and self-styled romantic, the man rocking-to-the-beat-of-a-different-drummer, the aforementioned Mr. Richman. Having grown up in Boston, I'd long been a devotee of the band and had followed Jonathan and the others from their earliest days doing free concerts on Cambridge Common near Harvard Square.

So it was more than a little thrilling to be asked to join a version of The Modern Lovers that featured – in the parlance of the day - the "chick singers."

One of those chicks was my friend, Ellie Marshall. Even then, Ellie was a serious singer deeply committed to life as a musician. She possessed a gentle, lilting, assured soprano and was itching to use it.

In contrast, I'd merely been a serious *fan* of rock and roll, a former college radio DJ, a denizen of local punk rock clubs like the Rat and Cantone's, a guitar player of minimal skill and an amateur singer with little significant experience to speak of. I was a dabbler. A hobbyist. My day job was writing scripts for a company that made industrial slide shows. It was, shall we say, a checkered lifestyle.

My pal Ellie had been hired by Jonathan as one of two backup singers for an upcoming West Coast tour of the newly forming Modern Lovers. The other singer (who shall go unnamed to spare her The Abject Shame!) was supposed to have taken her place in the band by now, singing alto harmony to Ellie's soprano. But early on it became blatantly obvious to Jonathan that the woman originally chosen apparently could *not* deliver one crucial ingredient in the band's sound.

It came down to this --- she could not satisfactorily clap her hands AND snap her fingers in one seamless move.

The horror.

One autumn afternoon, Jonathan laid it out to Ellie. He needed a replacement ASAP. Rehearsals were pending, followed swiftly by the tour.

What could be done?

As luck would have it, I lived downstairs from Ellie.

And yes, among my grab bag of talents? I COULD, indeed, clap my hands and snap my fingers in one seamless move.

Some might call it a superpower.

Ellie knocked on my door, stated the situation, and, once I calmed down, ushered me upstairs.

I nervously demonstrated my prowess, clapping and snapping my heart out.

I got the gig.

I felt obliged to ask if Jonathan wanted to actually hear me sing. He somewhat reluctantly said OK, as if it were some pesky detail that could just as easily not be addressed. And while the Judges might have given me higher scores in the Clapping and Snapping Division, Jonathan seemed happy enough with what he heard. And that is how I became a Modern Lover.

Two weeks after my hire I was singing on stage at the famed Roxy in Los Angeles. (This is when I learned the valuable lesson that acting as if you knew what you were doing was almost as good as knowing what you are doing.) A month into my tenure in the band we were in the pages of *Rolling Stone* (NOTE: Linda Ronstadt was on the cover. This reflects absolutely no glory on me. Strange bedfellows could be found 'neath the pages of the pop culture press, as true then as it is now). Not long after that we were recording at Capitol Studios in Hollywood. Sinatra, Nat King Cole and the Beach Boys all recorded there. The engineer for our early sessions had recorded the Beatles at the Hollywood Bowl. (Again, see previous comment about reflected glory.)

Still, being in this band was a dream I had not even dared to dream. I was quite literally in the right place at the right time with an adequate enough skill set. I felt guilty around my musician friends (including both my brother and my then-boyfriend) who were actively working toward music careers. Before Imposter Syndrome was a thing, I had fully felt it, sensing a profound unworthiness in my good luck.

But funny thing about luck. It changes. Almost inevitably. It did not take long for the glitzy early days to make way for what Jonathan characterized as the hardest touring he'd ever done in his career, before or since. The glamorous SRO gigs – the clubs in San Francisco and LA and NYC and DC - were merely bookends to all the sloggy, sparsely attended, spirit-crushing dates in places like Flint, Michigan and Rochester, NY and Champaign, Illinois. (What was the name of the joint where the rats were exterminated days before the gig and the stench of their rotting bodies hit right at showtime? I must be blocking.)

Yes, this journey had all the highs and lows and upside down moments of a Six Flags thrill ride. But it also had the mundane aspects of any job coupled with the weird problems that only rock and roll can present. Long days of driving. Being our own roadies. Collecting the money ourselves (once in a while unsuccessfully). Getting sick and ministering to sore throats and flu and sour stomachs brought on by road food with the power of pickled ginger and homemade vinegar/ cayenne tonics. Coping with the predictable internal strife as glorious promises dissolved our excitement into disillusioned bickering. Facing rejection as once-interested record companies vetoed Jonathan's musical choices. Watching as people who supposedly had our interests at heart snorted away the meager profits.

But in a way, I was oddly good with all that.

Those were dues that needed paying.

Being in the Modern Lovers taught me lessons about hard work and humility. About group dynamics and shady business practices. About resilience and the balm of friendship. And mostly about authenticity.

My "boss" Jonathan was (and still is) a legendarily quirky artist. He was often annoying with his iconoclastic pronouncements and capricious decision-making. But he is completely himself at all times and, to this day, presents that to his audiences every time he stands on stage. To be there beside him night after night and see him deliver his music with utter sincerity was a master class in living one's truth. He wasn't always popular. He wasn't always in phase with his fans. He wasn't always embraced with open arms. But he was genuine.

After three years in the band, lots of mileage and, finally, one major label album under our belts, I decided I should move on. Jonathan was already winnowing down the band, something that at first outraged me but now I see clearly as his prerogative as an artist. I didn't want to be fired. So I quit.

And in doing so, I began to turn my focus back to filmmaking. And really give myself to it. The way Jonathan gave himself to his music.

The early luck of my Modern Lovers' tenure was less evident in the world of film production. The breaks were not as easy to come by. But the lessons I'd learned about committing to your work and going all in stayed with me. I learned to find my voice with the topics I chose and the way I executed my films. Specifically my love of music and popular culture found new expression in the films I would end up making. Films about what it is like to live a musician's life. Films about the lesser known contributions of women musicians and musicians of color. Films about how art informs our culture and affects our historical arc.

As I continue my path in the film business, frustration still erupts, rejection still stings but I can see it better for what it all is – just part of the process. After decades of filmmaking, my vision is very much my own. Thanks to Jonathan I learned it is better to pursue that and fail than try to follow some predictable path and "succeed." I snapped and clapped my way into these realizations. For that I am very grateful. And you can put that in my obituary.

Beth Harrington is an Emmy-winning, Grammy-nominated independent producer, director and writer, born in Boston and transplanted to the Pacific Northwest. She most often focuses on work that explores American history, music and culture. Harrington's independent production *Welcome to the Club – The Women of Rockabilly*, a music documentary about the pioneering women of rock and roll, was honored with a 2003 Grammy nomination. This and other work reflects a long-standing love of music. She is a singer and sometimes guitarist, most noted for her years as a member of Jonathan Richman & The Modern Lovers on Sire Records. In 2014 her film *The Winding Stream* – The Carters, the Cashes and the Course of Country Music premiered at SXSW, later appearing in over 30 film festivals in the U.S. and abroad. Her latest projects include the documentary *Beyond the Duplex Planet* about artist David Greenberger, and a music-based feature film project, *The Musicianer.*

Harrington has also worked with public television stations WGBH in Boston and OPB in Portland producing, researching, and developing shows for both national and local air on series such as NOVA, Frontline, History Detectives, Oregon Art Beat and Oregon Experience. Her film *Fort Vancouver* received a NW Emmy for Best Historical/Cultural Program in 2019.

Omitted From My Obituary

"Empowering girls starts at home"

I Am

- Lisa Keohokalole Schauer

Standing there in the driveway, looking my daughter in the eye, I thought my heart was going to drop right out of my chest.

It had been a typical day until about 30 seconds ago. I'd run out of the office after work, trailed to the parking lot by an employee who needed just 10 more minutes. I sped to the grade school, continuing that conversation with the employee by phone all the way.

I had just a few minutes before I had to run out to the Empower Women + Girls community event, but I was committed to seeing my daughter during daylight hours, so I quickly bundled her into the car, and we used our 10 minutes of windshield time to review the plan for the evening:

Tennis lesson. Check. Dinner with Dad. Check. Then I'd be home at bedtime to tuck her in. All good.

We raced into the house, and I handed her over to her father like a relay baton, giving him a quick hello and see ya later.

Then my daughter asked, "Wait, where are you going now?"

"I'm going to an event about empowering girls," I answered, proud of the role model I was being for her.

Then she took my world apart in five simple words:

"Empowering girls starts at home."

I was stunned.

She continued,

"You haven't even seen me play tennis once this year."

I knew this was an important moment, and I was proud of her for using her voice, but the pain ran through my chest, making it difficult to breathe. I took a moment to find my voice, and check myself. So much for being a role model! I instantly revised my plans for the evening, and said,

"You're right. Let's go."

I watched her play tennis that night through tear-blurred eyes. And I reflected on who I'd become. Was I really a woman my daughter could be proud of? Was I a woman I could be proud of? How did I even get here? And, when it comes down to it, what does it really mean to be empowered as a woman?

I hate to even admit this ... but as a child, my favorite toy was Day-to-Night Barbie. She came with a pink, fold-out house that had an office on one side, and an apartment on the other. During the day, she wore a suit with high heels, carried a briefcase and sat at her desk ready to work. During the night, she had a fancy apartment where she lived by herself.

I thought if I could grow up to be Day-to- Night Barbie, I'd have it made.

She was my definition of feminine success. I strived to live her life, and I knew, even from a young age, that meant I needed to grow up to be economically independent. I would never let myself be dependent on anyone, especially a man. I had seen first-hand who lost in that scenario — the girl who gets married and she has a high school diploma, relies on a guy to support the family, something happens and girl is trapped because she can't financially take care of her children if she leaves him.

That trap was handed down to me, as I was forced to pass the potatoes at the dinner table to my abuser in exchange for ballet lessons and nice clothes. It wasn't that I didn't dream of my own Hallmark Channel version of Ken, I just knew I had to take care of myself first. I had to earn a college degree. Education was my path forward to an office of my own.

Despite my drive to achieve, nothing ever came easily to me. I wasn't the smartest person in the room. I wasn't the most athletic. I wasn't artistic, or musical. I was hard-working. I had a fierce commitment to working hard, figuring it out, and taking action. I didn't even really know what success meant, but I did know that I wasn't ever going to live in fear again, and I was willing to do anything to make that happen while not compromising my values.

And, honestly, that did a lot for me. I wowed people by doing what I said I would do, when I said I would do it. I researched, I planned, I said yes to small tasks and to big projects. During college when I was home for the summer, I worked at the corporate headquarters of Fred Meyer in the Public Affairs office. I was asked to flush every toilet in the giant corporate office with a stopwatch and spreadsheet timing how long it took for the water to flush. It didn't sound like anybody's idea of a good time ... but I leapt at the chance to prove my devotion to the work yet again.

I sincerely believe it was saying yes to flushing hundreds of toilets that led to an office with a bathroom and a view of Washington monument situated next to the Secretary of the Interior!

Pretty soon, people started to notice my work, and I developed a reputation for saying yes. During my internship that summer, I wrote press releases, I was on the local morning television show in the audience, I helped with golf tournaments collecting prizes and donations, I asked for a $10,000 gift from the Chief Operating Officer for the retail store Meier & Frank, I designed an internal employee newsletter and, of course, I flushed a lot of toilets.

I said yes and I worked hard. One of the women in the office was really good friends with a Director at the Department of Interior. She asked them for a favor — would they be willing to host me as an intern in DC during my senior year of college? They said yes. So, I landed my dream job in the inner office of the Secretary of Interior's office writing talking points on the potential Endangered Species Act listings of salmon in the Pacific Northwest ... all because I was willing to do whatever it took.

And, honestly, that became my default mode: to do whatever it took to get the job done. I got so caught up in the success, the achievements, the thrill of doing a hard job well, that I didn't even see the areas where I wasn't doing so well — things like being present for my child and truly walking my talk when it came to empowering women. That is, until Sydney's statement.

Over the course of the next year, I realized that while I had become Day-to-Night Barbie, she wasn't really my dream anymore. I didn't want a wardrobe of suits and a fancy apartment. I wanted a family. I wanted to belong. I wanted to beloved.

For a long time, I'd fooled myself into settling for something like that, minus the vulnerability. I believed I belonged at my company. I believed my partners were my brothers, and my co-workers were my friends. And while that was partway true, I had to come to the devastating realization that they meant much more to me than I did to them. They didn't need me in the same ways I so desperately needed them.

They actually had their own families, and I wasn't part of them.

Somewhere in my quest to achieve, I had lost sight of the most important people in my life. I was willing to negotiate family time in exchange for being available for the people that "needed" me at the office. The larger I grew the company, the more lives that depended on me, the more success I would achieve.

Sydney woke me up. After a significant amount of self-reflection and an inability to show up my best in my partnership, it was clear I needed to leave. My path to leaving my partnership was painful, and the scars are still visible. I was reaching towards my dream of love and belonging, though.

I had come a long way. But I still wasn't the woman or mother I wanted to be. I was empowering everyone around me, but not myself.

The time had come to own and share my story.

I am Lisa Teresa Kealohanui Tetunaui Keohokalole Schauer.

My first name, Lisa, was given to me by my adopted mother, Patricia. She is blond, 5′2″ and weighs about 100 pounds. It has always been obvious I was adopted with my brown skin, black hair, and larger, tall build.

My middle name, Teresa, was given to me by my biological mother, Melinda. This is my name on my original birth certificate.

My Hawaiian name is Kealohanui, which was given to me by my biological father, Adrian. The name honors me as the first born, and is my father's name, which signifies my place in order of importance.

My Tahitian name is Tetuanui and the name of my paternal grandmother's sister, a Tahitian royal name.

My father's last name is Keohokalole which represents the high Alis (or Royal Chiefs) in Hawaii. Keohokalole was the mother of the last living Queen, Liliuokalani.

And my married last name is Schauer.

I am a daughter who was raised by adopted parents. I am a daughter who met my biological mother in 2010 and my biological father in 2018. Both of my biological parents have welcomed me and have embraced me as their child. I know not many adopted children have a similar story of inclusion. I can only imagine how difficult it must be to meet your adult child. I remain grateful for their love and acceptance.

I am a child who was abused by my adopted father, who was forced to live with my abuser growing up in a household that pretended as though nothing ever happened.

I am a first-generation college graduate with not only two undergraduate degrees but a master's degree as well.

I am a wife to a man I love very much. I chose to marry a man over two decades older than me, falling in love with his kindness, empathy, and rock-solid integrity. While our age-difference surprises many, Al is my ideal life partner.

I am a mother to a 13-year daughter that gives me optimism and hope everyday as she reveals her commitment to kindness and serving others. She is incredibly empathetic and deeply feeling, she also has a voice she uses often that I know will serve her well as an adult! It took us three years, two miscarriages and two rounds of IVF before our beautiful Sydney was born.

I am "Granny Lisa." I will never forget the moment when two grade-school children in the back of our SUV on our way home from ice cream coined the phrase Granny Lisa. Obviously, I am way too young to be anyone's grandmother, which is why calling me Granny Lisa is just so funny (not)! When I married Al he had grown children and grandchildren. Growing up I was close to my grandparents and I knew the sacred bond that could form between grandchildren and grandparents. I also knew all of these children had "real" grandparents. So, I became Pop's wife, Lisa (and occasionally Granny Lisa). I hope these children know how proud I am to know them and to love them. They have been an absolutely amazing bonus to my life.

I am a sister. I have eight younger siblings. Seven of these siblings I met as an adult. All seven welcomed me by showing me I belonged. I cannot imagine this was easy for any of them and likely as shocking to them as it was to me. This pack of siblings has given me the connection and belonging I have so desperately needed. These siblings have also expanded my family to include their spouses, many of whom I feel deeply connected to!

I am an aunt. I have twelve nieces and nephews. They add laughter, love and joy to my life in ways I would never have imagined!

I am a friend. I have two friends who have been my sisters by love but not blood. I have known Staci since we were five years old and I have known Kari since she was born (she's a few years younger than me). While each offer support in different ways, they both remind me where I came from and what I have achieved. They are both fierce advocates. They center me and help me to be strong during the moments when I feel weak.

I am an entrepreneur who currently owns two businesses, one of which is a minority-led, woman-owned, small business.

I am a communicator. I believe in the power of telling story to connect, to listen to one another, to learn, and to lead.

I was a partner in an engineering and construction management firm before selling my shares in 2018. I was the first woman partner, the first woman Board Director, and the only non-technical partner in the firm's thirty-year history.

I am a serial volunteer in my community serving women, children, veterans and education causes close to my heart.

I am a Regent at Washington State University, appointed by Washington State Governor, Jay Inslee, to serve over 30,000 students, 2,500 faculty, and over 33,000
alumni.

And I am still growing.

Maya Angelo said, "Success is liking yourself, liking what you do, and liking how you do it."

My definition of success is a work in progress.

Today, success is taking and picking up my daughter from school multiple times throughout the week. I hear how her day went as soon as she gets in the car, instead of running through logistics and then only getting to see her again as she gets ready for bed. Success is working with my husband again. I have missed his insight and his energy in the work. Success is also finding time to set work aside. I am more present with my family than I've ever been before.

Success is learning to embrace the families that want to love me. These families may not all be connected by blood, but they are all connected by love. I am grateful to develop deep, trusting relationships with my family, my ohana. I am learning how to accept their love. I am learning to trust that I belong.

Success is embracing my Hawaiian culture and understanding the story of our people.

Success is forgiving myself and others when I am hurt. Success is letting the past not dictate my future.

Success is a client engagement with a lesser dollar value than in the past when I marketed and sold multi million dollar contracts, but it's exactly the right size for now. Success is building a team of communicators that care deeply about community, that are smart, talented, and partners in our work.

Success is living my dream of working with my business partner, Elizabeth to share women's stories, to gather women and to catalyze change.

Success is being brave enough to share my story, simply because it is my story.

Syndey was right: empowering women does start at home. But it doesn't end there.

We must all lift each other, see each other, and find ways to help each other uncover our unique definitions of success.

I am eternally grateful for the woman and the men who invested in me before I invested in myself, who believed in me before I knew how to believe in myself, who loved me and took me as one of their own when I didn't believe I was lovable or that I belonged. Our definitions of success should reflect our whole life and will be dynamic. Success is not simply an office, a title or money.

I, Lisa Teresa Kealohanui Tetunaui Keohokalole Schauer, am successful.

Lisa Keohokalole Schauer

drives with her shoes off, loves family trips to Disneyland, yellow cake with chocolate frosting, the simplicity of a Hallmark love story, spa days and serious retail therapy!

Lisa is the President of PointNorth Consulting, a values-based strategic communication and organizational development firm.

Lisa is called to serve her community. She believes her purpose is to radiate connection, to authentically bring people together. She currently serves as one of nine Regents for Washington State University, is a Board Director for the Columbia River Economic Development Council and a Board Director for the Society of Marketing Professional Services. She has served on the Boards of the Children's Center, Columbia Credit Union, Clark College Foundation, and the Association of Washington Businesses.

While recognition for her contributions makes Lisa uncomfortable, she has been humbled by the awards she has received including the Leonard Nadler Leadership Award from George Washington University, a Women of Influence award by the Portland Business Journal, an Iris Award from Clark College and an inaugural recipient of the Top 40 under 40 award from the Vancouver Business Journal. Lisa is a life-long learner who collects degrees and certifications in an effort to continually grow.

Lisa holds a Bachelor of Arts in Political Science, a Bachelor of Arts in Public Relations from Gonzaga University and a Master of Arts in Organizational Leadership and Learning from George Washington University.

"We are the authors of our story. My story changed because I confronted an ugly truth."

Twelve Steps - The Unexpected Gift

- Kelly Love

I am the author of my own story. If my life story was a book, it would have two sections; "before" and "after". My story has been punctuated by a single moment that changed the trajectory of my life. What I thought was the worst thing in the world that could happen to me, turned out to be the very best.

I am one of those women you hear about who has a problem with alcohol. We keep the big little secret from everyone, especially ourselves. I would never have called myself an alcoholic. I didn't think I fit the profile. No DUI's, no drinking on the job, no physical symptoms and I never blacked out. I liked my wine and the occasional vodka. I spent a few years as a non-drinker when I was pregnant and nursing. I didn't see alcohol as a problem for me. It was, I thought, a solution. I fancied myself a controlled drinker until a fateful night at the age of 36 that changed my life.

On that night, I went out drinking with friends. I had my customary three drinks. I have always counted my drinks. I have rules for myself about when, how much and where I can drink. On this night, I threw out my own rules. I had a fourth drink…maybe a fifth drink and I got drunk.

That is not my goal. I do not like the feeling of drunk. The room spins and my head feels thick. My goal is to feel good. I drink because I like the effect. I experience a warm, soothing, slightly fuzzy sensation from my head down to my toes. In this state, everything feels right within me. The things I think are wrong with me cease to exist. I am at ease and free from the strains and stress of the day. Alcohol quiets my brain.

In my 20 years of drinking, I could predict with some certainty that three drinks would produce the desired effect. Four drinks would be too much. If my words slurred, I knew I had overshot my goal.

For years, I relied on this calculation. I thought I had a good system that allowed me to enjoy alcohol without consequences. I thought I had beaten the game – I could control my drinking.

In my 30's, even though I would not admit it, my drinking had begun to change. I had gone through a divorce. It was a hard time and I felt a strong desire to drink to make the feelings of guilt and remorse fade. During my last year of drinking, I had switched from wine to vodka. I began drinking around the kids on my days off. I even took alcohol with me in the car WITH the kids taking them to soccer practice or to a matinee. I am ashamed I did that. Never would I ever want to do anything to harm my children. Yet, I did. More and more I reached for alcohol to smooth out the rough edges in my life. More and more I found myself irritable, restless and discontent without it. Alcohol was taking control my life.

So on the night of January 30, 2000, it should come as no surprise to anyone reading this that after leaving my friends; I stopped at one more bar for one more drink. I was still feeling irritable, restless and discontent. My earlier drinking had not produced the desired effect. I had that drink and knew I had crossed the line. I was drunk as I left the bar walking back to my car around one a.m. Unbeknownst to me a stranger from the bar followed me and attacked me. With no defenses and without my wits about me, I was easy prey. I did not call the police or go to the hospital. I could not, would not, tell another soul: my shame too great. I went to work that morning, anchored the morning news, made simple chitchat with the weatherman and tried to bury the secret so no one would ever know.

Within a few days, the bruises gave me away. My loved ones were distraught. I had no good explanation as to why I was there and why I was drunk. In that dark painful place, I realized I couldn't drink like that ever again. I also knew eventually, I would. I couldn't imagine my life without alcohol.

For the first time, I could clearly see the ugly truth. I had a problem with alcohol.

I decided I would do what my father had done. I knew about twelve step recovery programs because of my dad. I had been to meetings with him. He got sober when I was 13. I knew it had saved his life.

Never had I ever imagined I would need it too. It's the last place I wanted to go. I didn't want to admit defeat. I desperately didn't want to be an alcoholic. But I didn't have any other bright ideas. I had no clue how to fix this. Looking back, I can see I had been given the gift of desperation; willing to concede I needed help.

I tip toed into my first meetings, hoping no one would see me. They welcomed me warmly with strong coffee and bad jokes. But I'm wasn't sure yet I fit in. By the third meeting on the third day, I heard a woman speak. I could relate to everything she said. I decided to allow myself the chance to stay. I attended many meetings. The first time I said the words "I'm an alcoholic", I actually felt relief, rather than being judged or shamed. In some strange way, I felt like I'd come home. I experienced acceptance, belonging and love.

These new friends laughed at the strangest things; sharing their misadventures, heartaches and triumphs. I found them to be disarmingly honest and vulnerable in what they shared. These sober men and women of all ages and from all walks of life who would not normally mix had clearly found a solution to their drinking problem through this simple program where one alcoholic helps another, united by their common foe.

End of story? I thought so. But it was just the beginning. When I got sober I expected to feel better right away. In some ways, I actually felt worse. I felt all kinds of negative emotions and I didn't have alcohol to medicate. I realized I had not developed healthy coping skills during my years of drinking. I was in many ways, emotionally immature. I hated that diagnosis as much as I disliked the alcoholic diagnosis. Luckily, a woman named Julia showed up on my path. She pointed to the twelve steps of recovery and put me on the path.

Step One says "We admitted we were powerless over alcohol and our lives had become unmanageable." I was not convinced I was powerless; not at first. I still had my job and my family. On the outside, my life looked manageable. How could I make this admission? You may have heard the saying that every alcoholic needs to hit bottom before they can get help. Was this really my bottom or was it just a bad night?

In Step One, I wrote out my drinking history – all of it. Prior to this writing exercise, I would have told you that I drank like everybody else. I would have conveniently forgotten large chunks of my drinking past. In writing out my drinking history, I was shocked to see all the close-calls, the embarrassments and the impulsive decisions that seemed to permeate my life. Now I could begin to see the unmanageability. For the first time I could also see how I was drinking more, not less. I could see the progression. I could see that if I continued on, I would get worse not better. I could see that alcohol had power over me and eventually I would lose the things and people I hold most dear in my life. I became convinced: I am an alcoholic. It does not define who I am, but it is important for me to claim it every day and I do so with a grateful heart. It was the price of admission to my sober, happy life.

At Step Two, I balked. In order to stay sober, I would need a power greater than myself. I would need a relationship with a higher power." I would have to become willing to shed my self-reliance peeling back the layers of an onion and learn to trust God. Raised Catholic I knew there was a God but he seemed very far away. As a child, I believed God did not care about the things going on in my home. I believed we were not worthy of his protection and care. I chose to rely on myself not God. My next encounter with God would be years later when my firstborn son died of meningitis. For a moment, I felt his presence. But I also felt a condemnation that I was to blame and I blamed God. Over the years, I had made attempts to connect spiritually but always retreated driven by a false belief that I fell outside God's care.

So, when I saw Step Two, my heart sank. How could I grab onto such a flimsy reed – I didn't yet trust God to provide care and protection. I'm so grateful I was given the dignity of my process in this very personal work. No one told me what to believe or what it should look like. In Step Two, I was given grace to create my own relationship with a God of my understanding. I was encouraged to look for evidence of God in my life through the people he put on my path along the way. I learned over time, through experience, that as I move out of isolation and connect with others, I find God is working in my life and that he wants to use me to help others. I'm happy to report our relationship continues to grow.

Step Three looked simple to me. I was to turn my will and my life over to the care of God as I understand him. Simple – but not easy. I had no idea until that moment how much I tried to control people, places and things in my life. I was reluctant to give up that control to my higher power. I thought my self-sufficiency was a good thing and it protected me from getting hurt. It's taken years for me to let down my guard and allow my higher power to be in charge. I still need daily reminders or as I call them, surrenders, to let God in. I am a work in progress to be sure.

By the time I take Step Four, I had been sober for six months. I am amazed and excited to see glimpses of my new sober life. I am active in meetings, I have a few sober friends and I have a new sense of purpose for my life. But I am still plagued by frequent negative emotions. My sponsor shows me how to make a searching and fearless moral inventory of myself and then share it with her as suggested in Step Five.

It's a simple process. I write out my resentments, my fears and my harms. It helps me identify the core instincts that drive the behaviors that have caused damage in my most important relationships. It shines a light on my character assets and defects. I can see how my instincts for protection and emotional security have over driven my thoughts, emotions and actions causing problems in my life. I get to take responsibility for my part rather than blame other people. The best part of the inventory is that it provides a way forward to heal old hurts and challenge old beliefs. I start to see how I've allowed my past to dictate my future. It's a starting point for transformative change.

Steps Six and Seven build on the previous steps – cultivating my character assets and asking God to help remove those defects that take away from my usefulness in the world. I continue to learn in this process I am neither a terrible person or a perfect person. I begin to understand the concept of being "right-sized" and with that, comes a tremendous peace.

Steps Eight and Nine require action. Who have I wronged and how do I make amends? My sponsor led me through this process to ensure that my side of the street is clean and that I own up to the damage I have caused my family and my fellows. There can be no excuses or justifications. The tricky part about making an amends is to let go of any expectation that the other person will forgive me or the relationship will be restored. What I like most of all about this step is the "living amends" that I get to make every day to my parents, my children, my employer and my friends. I get to be fully present, engaged, and consider their needs before mine. I have been selfish in many ways, putting my needs first. The living amends gives me a chance to become a better daughter, parent, partner, employee and friend.

Step Ten is a daily practice like so many of these twelve steps. It's like sweeping the kitchen floor; best done regularly so dirt doesn't build up. It asks me to take a personal inventory on a daily basis and promptly make things right when I've done wrong. Maybe I've told a lie, been impatient or unkindly gossiped about another. The daily inventory gives me a chance to see it and address it, hopefully that same day. Keeping the slate clean helps keep my spirit light.

Step Eleven like Step Three is my favorite step. It asks me to pray and to mediate to know God's will for me. My brain is still very busy and I get caught up in the clamors of the world, which makes it hard to get quiet and listen for my higher power. I still want to run way out ahead of God and show him all my great ideas. But I'm learning to pause and let him guide me rather than me try to guide him.

Step Twelve asks me to take the principles of the program and try my best to practice them with my family and in my community. I also get to reach out to other alcoholics to offer them what was so freely given to me. Over the years I've been lucky to work with amazing women who like me, have recognized their problem with alcohol and who want to learn to live life on life's terms; living their best lives. Together we share heartaches and joys. We know each other inside out. We have found true connection, belonging and love.

Being sober has become second nature to me but I am not cured. What I have is a daily reprieve. I don't avoid situations where alcohol is present. I don't feel deprived when I'm around people who drink. It's not an issue for me as long as my spiritual house is in order. In my 20 years of sobriety I have experienced a handful of moments where I have wanted to drink. Once in a while, I have entertained the thought that perhaps I can drink like a normal person. I cannot afford to entertain that lie. I know what to do: say a prayer, call a friend and if need be, remove myself from the situation. Over the years I have seen sober friends who believed they could drink like normal people and relapsed. Some of them never regain the sobriety they once had.

Whereas I used to plan events and trips to include alcohol, I have learned I can do anything I want to do without a drink and actually have more fun. I can go to a happy hour and enjoy the conversation. The difference now is that I go home after the second diet coke.

I don't consider alcohol to be a bad thing or a good thing. I do not assign it a value; negative or positive. I don't begrudge anyone their right to drink. I am not on a crusade to get people to quit. I am hopeful we, as a culture, can move this conversation out into the light where we can share our experiences and support one another. We are the authors of our story. My story changed because I confronted an ugly truth. What I thought was the worst thing that could have ever happened to me has turned out to be the very best.

Kelly Love grew up in Seattle and early on developed a passion for journalism. At the age of 20, she went to work as a television news reporter at KTVB TV in Boise. Idaho.She spent 20 years in the broadcast industry as a reporter and anchor; at KUTV in Salt Lake City and KGW in Portland Oregon. In 2005 she went to work for then U.S. Representative Brian Baird serving as his District Director. After his retirement in 2010, Kelly went to work as CEO at the Greater Vancouver Chamber of Commerce. In 2015, Kelly joined Legacy Salmon Creek Medical Center in community and media relations. In 2019, she left Legacy to become the Chief Communications Officer at Clark College.

Kelly has two children, Eric and Sarah, now grown. When Sarah went to first grade, Kelly returned to college to complete her bachelor's degree and graduated from WSU-Vancouver in 2003.

Kelly's community involvement includes volunteer service on numerous non profit boards. She currently serves as Board Chair at Columbia Credit Union.

She remains active in her community and shares a passion for fishing with her soon-to-be husband Steve. They live in La Center.

"It is sometimes better to help others succeed over winning."

The Athlete

- Alishia Topper

From the moment of my birth, I've been an athlete.

Every fiber of my being, every molecule of my body and mind, every single thing I have been or will be, all comes back to that.

In some ways, it feels like I've been running all my life. It's only now, as I move into my early 40s, that I'm learning how to embrace all the elements of my race.

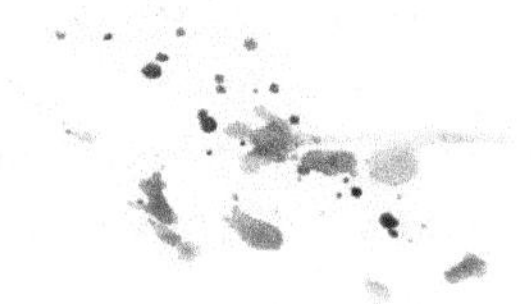

My race started on May 15, 1978, when I shot out of the womb with one arm punched straight ahead, and went from suckling to running, with no crawling in between. That's the story according to my mother, Cheri, at least. She'd say as a toddler I was always slightly out of control, tipped forward with gravity controlling my pace. It was my abnormally long toes gripping the ground like a raptor's talons holding a fish that kept me from what should have been catastrophic tumbles.

It seems like I came into this world prepared for what I was going to find in it — a lot of adversity.

My mom was just fourteen when she became pregnant with me, kicked out of her home by her mother, just over fifteen and a ward of the state of Oregon when I was born, in the care of the Salvation Army.

My birth certificate has a blank space where my father's name should be located.

Just a year and a half later, my mom gave birth to my sister, Heather. She was only sixteen when she married our father, one of the worst mistakes of her life. He ended up doing profound damage to her and our family, leaving scars that persist to this day. By the time she was 19, she was a teenage mother of two, with an eighth-grade education, determined to not just survive but be strong willed and wild. The grit, strong will, and resilience that got her through that runs through me too.

I knew things were bad pretty early on. It would be hard not to, given the combination of domestic violence, absentee parenting, profanity, violence, and drug use. But, in the way of people who grow up in those circumstances, it was all I knew. In my mom's own way, she made me feel loved. I felt like I belonged. And yet, something kept driving me, kept gnawing at me.

That fear kept me competitive, sometimes to an unhealthy degree. As a scrappy fourth grader, all of 4'2 and 60 pounds, I would challenge the boys to playground competitions over and over again, reveling in how I could beat them all. Enjoying it even more when they were rude and mean to me, and then I ran them into the ground.

When my mom fell madly in love with her new boyfriend, Doug, I thought things might get better, though looking back now, I probably should have known better. Doug was a tall, dark, and handsome former minor league baseball player, who lost twin babies at birth. They were born deformed with six fingers and toes. He never recovered or had children after that and drank Hamms beer from morning until night. Despite this, he was my biggest sports fan.

As a sixth grader, I had found track and field, and was completely enamored with it. Doug and my mom came to every track meet, and hearing their voices in the crowd made me swell with pride. While our home life was filled with conflict and arguments, at track meets, there was unity. There were undeniable facts — the time of a race was the time of a race, whoever won had won, and there was a stopwatch to prove it. No arguments, no violence. Just competition.

Of course, this was also the same year Doug pressured my mom to get pregnant, because he wanted a baby. The same year she started sneaking birth control pills, terrified that he would find out. The same year our periodic fleeing of the house intensified to every night going to sleep in the car to avoid his abuse and violence.

She used to say to me and my sister Heather, "Learn from my mistakes and be better than me." Even now, I still look back at what she was going through, the strength it took, and how she imparted that to me, and feel admiration and love for her. She called my sister and I her "bird girls", and wanted to keep us in her nest, keep us as safe as she could, even when that wasn't very safe at all.

The abuse went on for years before she finally got up the courage to pack up our things and take us out of this situation. A few months later, she was married again, this time to a man she met at a bar. She moved us to Amboy, Washington, and three years later I moved out. I was still her bird girl, but in her eyes, I was an adult now. I had to leave the nest. I was just sixteen years old.

And so, I ran.

I ran into athletics and away from Doug's fists, and all the times we'd been evicted, from my mom's marriage, which ended in divorce when the man she married was incarcerated for statutory rape of a minor, and from her rebound boyfriend who was a cokehead, and using her. I got even more competitive, even more determined.

No one could see all those sleepless nights, and how they were adding up and tipping my scale towards failure. No one could see how every day, as I ran towards a positive path, my life story grew more unique and unlikely. I just believed I was tough and I was determined, believed it so hard it became true.

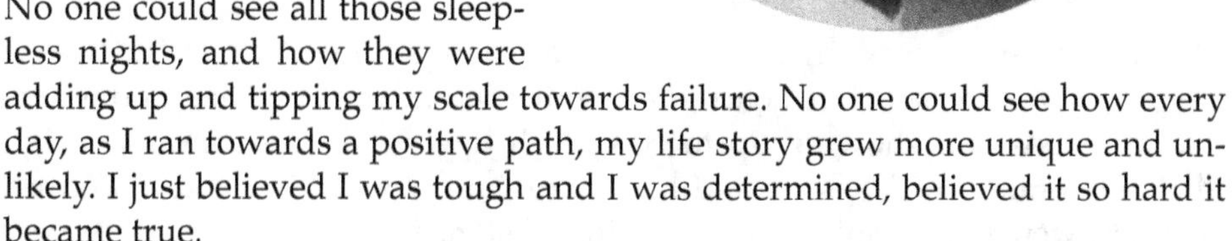

Then, something amazing happened.

I was couch-surfing with friends, when I met Spencer, my boyfriend, and more importantly, his mom Cheryl.

Cheryl saw potential in me, and took me into their home. She treated me like a daughter, and for the first time, that came with rules, boundaries and educational expectations, instead of my mom's blind love and living in uncertainty. Life was completely different there. While I had initially gotten into the same co-dependent tendencies of my mother with Spencer, Cheryl helped me grow. She was amazing, and strong, helped me learn about computers, and took me on college visits. She and her husband had two sons, and lived in a beautiful house, and while things weren't perfect, they worked at their relationship. Even when things were at their worst, they talked. And for someone much more used to hitting, this was amazing to me.

I started being able to see a path forward. The competition became more than just running away, I started running towards something — a future I would have never thought possible.

It was around this time that I also met Coach Piper, my high school track and field coach. She truly believed in me, the way you dream a coach would. She knew I had a challenging life, but didn't let me use it as an excuse. Instead, she helped me overcome adversity, and made sure I showed up to practice every day, pushing me further than I thought I could go.

You see, I had always thought I was a sprinter and a jumper, and that was that. Coach Piper, however, saw a distance runner in me, and kept pressuring me to come out with that team. I kept refusing, but she wouldn't let it die. Fall came around, and every day, I would run into her in the hall, or at gym class, and she would encourage me to join the cross-country team because it would make me a better track athlete. What she saw that I didn't was that as a sprinter, I could just run cross country and call it training without being a distance runner. It was all psychological, and I finally broke down and showed up for practice.

Running cross-country my sophomore year changed my life forever. I wasn't very good that season, but Coach Piper didn't let me miss practice, and it gave me a purpose for showing up to class each day. I still competed in sprints that sophomore track season and had marginal success. My mindset and my strength were being molded into a middle-distance runner. By my junior year, I ran my first 800 meter race, and that changed everything.

A year later, I was sitting on Cheryl's couch meeting with coaches and college recruiters from all over the country. I had developed into a great 800 meter track athlete, and was determined to get to college on a running scholarship, but hadn't made the times yet for a full ride.

It only took one race, one qualifying time, to plant the stride toward my dream of college. I spent the day and evening before the meet in the delivery room with Heather. She was giving birth to her first daughter, Merissa. She was only sixteen, and I became an aunt at seventeen. With little sleep, I wanted to miss class and skip the track meet that evening. Coach Piper wouldn't even consider it. So I suited up, and with harnessed emotions, exhaustion, and my competitive defiance, I ran fast enough to qualify for districts and on to the Washington State Championship meet. It was euphoric, and unbelievable. That race set me up to run a record time of 2:10.81 and earn a top ten fastest high school time in the country and my ticket to college.

I had tremendous personal growth and positive relationships in college.The experiences led to me earning All-American honors in the 800 meters, and qualifying for the Olympic Trials. I am who I am today because of these experiences, Cheryl and Coach Piper and sports. Without knowing it, Cheryl and Coach Piper had helped me open doors to an unbelievable future of college, professional career, and public service.

Earning both my bachelor's degrees, and then my master's opened up the world for me, and let me see that I actually could make positive changes in the world. I became heavily involved in issues like youth homelessness, affordable housing policy, and multimodal transportation policy, focusing on cyclists and pedestrians, and found myself uniquely placed to contribute because of my life's experiences — but I never would have gotten there without their help.

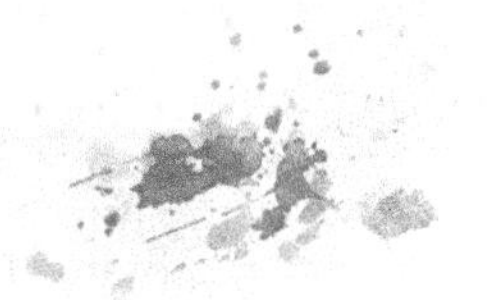

Now, all these years later, I'm settling into my early forties and finally recognizing, acknowledging, and accepting my unique strengths and positive influence. I'm no longer running from the idea of being driven, hard-working, and competitive, I'm embracing it. And, I'm learning to embrace my vulnerability, and the fact that there's always going to be a better version of myself.

It's a daily struggle. Part of me wants the race to be won, wants to know that I've reached my full potential. But the athlete in me loves the struggle, loves that this race will never be over, until I die. I'm a competitor at heart, an athlete to my core. I will live and die with my experiences, my failures, and my successes. My life is about outsprinting adversity, and I plan on winning the race.

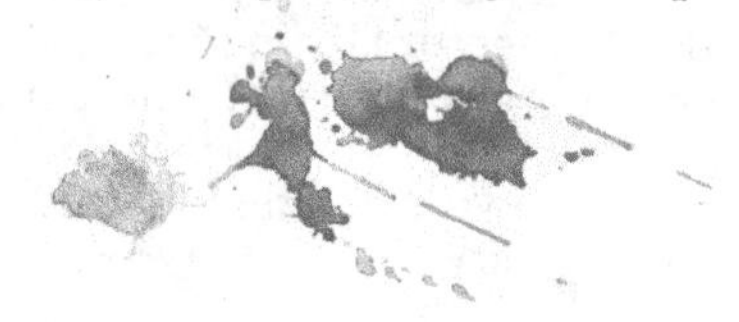

Alishia Topper was born and raised in the Pacific-Northwest. She attended Battle Ground High School and graduated from Washington State University-Pullman in 2000 earning a BS in psychology and BA in foreign languages and literatures. She earned a Master's Degree in public administration from Portland State University.

Alishia is an American public administrator and politician who has served as Clark County Treasurer since 2019. Serving as a non-partisan, she also served five years on the Vancouver, Washington City Council from 2014-2018.

As a city councilmember, Alishia embraced her responsibility and earned the title of "Advocacy All-Star" from the Association of Washington Cities for her hard work in advancing policy solutions for homelessness and affordable housing. She was also appointed by Governor Jay Inslee and unanimously confirmed by the Senate to serve on the state's Housing Finance Commission.

Prior to being elected to office, Alishia worked for Vancouver Public Schools advocating for low-income and homeless students. She was recognized by the Greater Vancouver Chamber of Commerce as one of Clark County's Most Interesting People of 2014. Alishia was a nominee for Washington State University-Vancouver's 2013 Women of Distinction, and named by the Vancouver Business Journal as a 2011 Accomplished and Under 40.

Alishia and her husband Ryan, were married in May 2006 and have two cats, Marvin and Sir Humphrey Hillary.

"I like to believe it
was just a
little miracle.
Most of all
I credit my mom."

"There is no such thing as failure, there's just giving up too soon."

-Jonas Salk, developed the first successful polio vaccine

It's the smell. That wet wool, old-sock smell. Even just a faint whiff jolts me back to my younger days. The room was cold, the lights were dim. I was tightly wrapped in a warm, heavy scratchy blanket. I tried to lift my arms. I just couldn't move. Someone was beside me, so I was not alone. I was not scared.

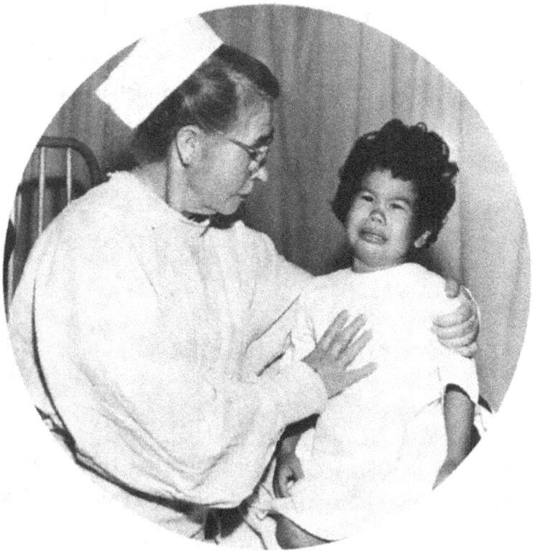

Growing up in Honolulu in the mid-1950s was easy as a middle-class family. Dad worked for the family business and mom stayed at home with me and my infant sister. Mom was pregnant with my brother.

We took afternoon walks to the water tower in our neighborhood—my hand barely reaching up to hers. My mom called me her "ray of sunshine." At nearly 3-years old, I remember a happy, simple life.

Things were about to change.

"Can you move your arm?" asked my pediatrician.

Just a few weeks after the land- mark press conference announcing success of the vaccine trials, an Idaho doctor reported a case of paralytic polio in a recently vaccinated girl. Over the next few weeks, similar reports trickled in. A California laboratory produced defective, live virus vaccines. All involved a disturbing detail: paralysis began in the vaccinated arm, rather than in the legs as was more common.

Thousands of children became ill and hundreds were permanently paralyzed.

It was a scary time. I was immediately admitted to the hospital; my sister came down with the polio fever and my mom worried about possible exposure to her unborn child.

I vividly remember frantically reaching for my parents. Someone was holding me back. A glass window separated us. Paralyzed and in isolation, I cried.

Being in quarantine meant no contact with my family. It's odd. I only remember being happy there. While in the hospital, doctors scooped me up in their arms for their morning rounds. I talked a lot, so I made friends with many other sick, isolated kids.

Compared to some other children, I was the lucky one. Months of daily hot wool blanket compresses and physical therapy worked.

No one will ever know why or how I regained most of my muscle tone and strength. I like to believe it was just a little miracle. Most of all I credit my mom. During my rehab, she was adamant that no one treat me like an invalid. She instilled the strong belief that "I can do anything!" She encouraged me to just "go with it." Life moves on.

Resilient. Confident. Happy.

Sometimes I wonder. If I didn't contract polio, perhaps I would not be the person I am. So, here's to you mom. You made me believe in the best of everything.

Rhona Sen Hoss

Happy ♡ Aloha

Life is short so I'm smiling while I've still got my teeth.

Looking to raise a family in a not-so-expensive city like Honolulu, we landed in Vancouver, WA in the early-1980s. My hubby and I raised our two sons in this welcoming, caring community. So blessed to work in many great local organizations like SWIFT, The Columbian, Washington State University Vancouver and even statewide in the Office of Governor Inslee. Honored to be recognized as a Woman of Achievement, 100 of the Most Powerful Women in Clark County and for 10-years served on the Clark College Board of Trustees. Life is good traveling the world, having the love of family and lifelong friends—I'm grateful every day.

"I tried not to squelch her natural feistiness knowing she would need it to deal with the White world."

Survived by my Daughter

- PAM OSBORNE

My obituary will not say I was infertile…barren. That will erase ten years of my life… ten years of not being able to do what women are uniquely capable of doing—propagate the species… ten years of taking my basal cell temperature before climbing out of bed in the morning and being hypervigilant about ovulation pain…ten years of making love by the calendar regardless of whether the spirit moved...ten years of lying in bed in various positions after sex trying to give the little wigglers the best chance of finding their target… ten years of painful tests and procedures sitting in waiting rooms with pregnant women… ten years of dreading going to the mall because I'd have to see other women with their swollen baby-bodies...ten years of being furious if those pregnant women were smoking or yanking a child's arm impatiently.

I dreaded Mother's Day for those ten years. People, in general, were not terribly sympathetic. "Want kids? Take mine!" they'd quip. Fellow church members counseled somberly, "If God had wanted you to be a mother, you'd have gotten pregnant." My mother said, "I don't see you as a mother; I see you as a career woman." Having been a stay-at-home mother herself, she couldn't imagine combining a career with motherhood. But I ached to become a mother. When I was a child, my girlfriends and I daydreamed about how many children we wanted. Iintended to have at least three. My first husband had a child from a previous marriage and was ambivalent about starting another family; so when we could no longer stand the monthly emotional roller coaster and the invasive medical procedures, we decided to remain child free. I had been wanting to transition from being a school media specialist to being a medical librarian, so I put my energy into a career change. I commuted up to the University of Washington each week to take an additional required course, did a practicum in a hospital library, took some medical vocabulary classes, and…got terribly depressed. I went to a therapist who counseled, "It seems to me that if you decided to become child free and you are this miserable, you'd better rethink your decision." I went home, sat my husband down, and declared, "I *have* to have a child, or I am not going to survive." We called an adoption agency.

Being infertile condemns you to a lifetime of sitting with groups of women who are never together long before they feel compelled to tell each other how long they were in labor with each child they birthed. They dismiss me with, "Oh, you did it the easy way—you adopted." I roll my eyes at them. My husband and I had to share our private medical records with the adoption agency to *prove* we were unable to have a biological child. We had to be fingerprinted at the police station and submit to criminal background checks done. We had to supply bank records to prove that we could financially support a child. We had to have a social worker come to our house to interview us and check to see if we had the proper environment in which to raise a child. We had to supply references from friends and family testifying that we would be responsible parents. I have often wondered how different the world would be if all potential parents had to go through such scrutiny.

Several months after we had agency approval, we received a letter from them with a couple photos of a two-month baby girl asking if we would accept her. We said yes immediately and within days got a phone call telling us that the baby could arrive in as little as two weeks. It was mid-May, and I was a school librarian at the time. I went into high gear trying to get the books collected from the students and inventoried as soon as possible not wanting to leave that for a substitute to do. The two weeks passed. Baby did not arrive. The school year ended, and an empty summer began. I grieved each day that passed with my baby in another woman's arms half a world away. In late June we got word that a substitute official, who did a last-minute health check before the baby was to be put on a plane to the US, denied her passage because he didn't believe that we knew about two tiny birthmarks she had. The orphanage had, in fact, sent pictures of the marks and we had approved them formally. Nevertheless, we had to wait for official papers to be snail-mailed to us from

Korea. We signed on their dotted lines and snail-mailed them back. Our daughter finally arrived on August 2nd at five ½ months old. I figure my labor lasted 2½ months; my pregnancy, eleven. So much for "easy."

My obituary will not say that my daughter is adopted. Occasionally I see that information in an obituary and do not understand why. Isn't your child *your child* regardless of how they came to the family? Garrison Keillor tells a Lake Wobegon story of the Tollerude family adopting a Korean baby. When the story was written, people could still go to the gate at the airport to meet an incoming plane so the whole Tollerude family watches on tiptoe as a volunteer carries their baby toward them on a jetway. "And that's the way all babies arrive," the story concludes, "they come down a chute!" When people ask me, "Don't you have any children of your own?" I say, "My daughter *is* my own." They stare at me in confusion. I make no attempt to explain.

My obituary will not say that my daughter's race differs from mine. Lots of people have children who have different color hair or eyes or a dissimilar body build. My daughter and I are unalike in most every way. We do not blend in. When she was an infant, strangers felt free to approach us and ask questions that were invasive, intrusive and sometimes ignorant. "How will you understand her…she'll speak Korean!" was a common one. ["Babies learn the language they hear spoken around them. She'll speak English because that's what we speak."] "Where are her *real* parents?" was another. ["You mean her birth parents? My husband and I are her real parents. We are the ones raising her."] In general, I tried to educate rather than react, but not always…like the time a woman stomped up to me in the mall while I was pushing my baby in a stroller and demanded, "Just what exactly does your husband look like?" "What does *yours* look like," I snapped and kept walking while I shook with rage. Another common reaction was to credit us as heroes of some type for adopting. "Where is she from? What a wonderful thing you did adopting her!" I protested, "I didn't do it for her. I did it for me. I needed her." They didn't believe me. I didn't feel at all heroic; I felt selfish. I wondered if we had done the right thing taking her out of her own country, away from people who looked like her, away from her culture and heritage. Should we have given her a first name that went with our Swedish surname rather than keeping her Korean name? Would an American name help her fit in better or would her Korean name have been preferable to honor her roots?

When she was a toddler and beginning to learn the words for the parts of the body, she would stab a stubby finger in my eye, and I could tell already she knew her eyes didn't look like mine. I'd stand her on the bathroom counter, and we'd look in the mirror and talk about what was similar and what was different. Our eyes were shaped differently, but we both had two of them; our hair was a different color, but we both had some covering our head; and so forth. When she was four, she announced, "I hate my hair and my eyes." "Is that because they don't look like Mama's?" I asked. "Yes," she answered and went back to her Legos. When she was no longer connected to me by a stroller or a hand, I had to introduce myself as her mother at doctor visits, school conferences, child birthday parties, etc. Once I was called to pick her up from the school health room and was led to the blond, blue-eyed child waiting there. Sometimes it was my daughter who did the introducing. One day a new friend came over to play. My daughter greeted her at the door saying, "That's my mom. I'm adopted. Let's play!"

At age two my husband and I walked her through the naturalization process where she became a United States citizen. Had we failed to do so, she could have been called up to serve in the Korean military. When the adoption became final, we received a Washington State birth certificate for her to replace the Korean one. I didn't think to carry it with me, but there were times when it would have been handy. Once when we were going to Victoria BC for the day, we were in line for the 6am ferry. The friend that drove us there asked if I had her birth certificate with me. It took a minute for me to realize why I might need one, and then I got angry. Other people don't have to carry proof of parenthood with them. Why should I? I didn't want to admit there could be a problem. I stomped into the ferry office. The officials there said, "No problem. We'll let her leave the country. Just be forewarned that she might not be able to get back in without any proof she's your daughter. We're concerned about child trafficking." We did not go to Victoria BC that day.

Several years after my first husband and I divorced, I began dating a man who went to my church but attended a different service. We bumped into each other one Sunday morning when my daughter was with me. I saw him do a double-take when I introduced them and realized I hadn't mentioned to him she was Korean. It hadn't occurred to me. She was simply my daughter. In those days I used to say with pride, "I forget that she doesn't look like me." What I realize now with great humility is that statement is a form of white privilege… as though the love I have for her as a parent is able to blind me to all our differences and render me incapable of appreciating how our obvious differences play out in her life. Having a child of a minority has exposed me to racial prejudice in ways that most White People are incapable of seeing.

When my daughter was about three, we were away at a family work camp. At breakfast I saw my daughter sitting at the adjoining table next to a seven-year-old who was teaching her to pull up and down at the corners of her eyes in imitation of the shape of Asian eyes. I felt sick to my stomach. I spoke to the girl who was unaware that she had done anything inappropriate and later to her mother who was horrified and embarrassed. They didn't intend any harm. They were White. Racial prejudice is insidious. Weeks later my daughter and I sat down to have lunch in a grocery store deli area. I had forgotten to get silverware. She wanted to get it for us, so I let her walk across the room by herself to get it. I glanced over and saw an old man glaring with hatred at my darling, innocent child. I'm sure he assumed she was unattended since he didn't connect us visually and the look on his face said he thought she was stealing the silverware.

For my daughter it has been a lifetime of people asking rudely, "Where are you from?" She learned to smile and say, "Vancouver" even though she knew that the question they intended to ask and didn't know how was "What nationality are you?" Watching my daughter struggle with it, I have learned never to ask that question.

When she began dating, she announced, "I'm not attracted to Asian men." I realized she thought of herself as White—*bananas* or *twinkies* they are called in the world of prejudice—yellow on the outside and white on the inside. In her late twenties she married an Amerasian. Part of what drew them together was the bond they shared of their experiences of bias. She can tell him things she wouldn't tell me—in part to protect me from her pain, but also because she knows I wouldn't understand. There's a donut shop just a few blocks from where I live. A group of elderly retired men congregate there to drink coffee and chat each morning. Recently my daughter and her husband went there. They came home fuming—sure that those men were biased against them, uncomfortable under their unwelcoming stares. I wanted to say, "They stare at everyone that way," but I didn't. I don't know. I don't have a lifetime of being stared at like they have, and it's a microaggression for me to challenge their experience.

They now have an infant son, so a new chapter is unfolding for us all. They tried for a long time before it happened and had started thinking about adoption; but my daughter wanted a birth child very badly. She has asked me multiple times, "Who do you think he looks like?" I know she wants to hear that he looks like her. She's had a lifetime of not looking like anyone in the family. Recently I said to her, "I'm thrilled that you now have people in your family that look like you." "Yes," she said. "I always wanted to look like someone in the family. But as badly as I wanted that, I never felt like I didn't *belong* to the family. I'm not sure that sending me to Korean Culture Camp made me get in touch with the culture all that much, but I very much appreciated the effort you made to get me there." I wish she and her family lived closer. They live north of Seattle and work in downtown. But I am happy to have them there where there are more Asians and away from Portland with its history of racial prejudice. I want them safe. Her Korean mother-in-law has offered to take them to Korea someday

to meet family over there and see the country. It is something I can't give her, and I am happy for her to have the opportunity though I must admit it makes me a little jealous. I have read that adult adoptees have a hard time when they travel there because they don't know the culture and don't speak the language, but they look like they should. It can make them feel like they don't belong anywhere. However, they'll be sheltered by being with family, and I am grateful.

In a book club I belong to, we read a novel last year about the Japanese internment in the United States during World War II. I have read several books on the topic, and this one was more about the day-to-day life in the camp. One person in the group said she didn't think it would have been too bad for the children because they had others to play with during the day and it was just part of life. "Would you want your grandchildren playing in the desert in a guarded razor-wired camp?" I asked her. She looked confused. We White people can't imagine anything like that happening to us. But I worry about what will happen to my daughter and her family if we ever go to war with North Korea. Would history repeat itself that way? I swear if it did I would go with them. No one can convince me it could never happen. History is on my side, and the "us" versus "them" feeling is stronger than ever in this country.

Sometimes I look back and wonder if adopting her was a good idea with all she's experienced. I feel guilty for taking her away from her culture and her people; however, at the time of her birth, single pregnant women in Korea did not receive any family or societal support. Had she been raised there, she would not have been on the family register of her father's name and, therefore, would not have been educated beyond the sixth grade or been eligible to work.

What I know is that I *had* to have a child. I tried to give her a strong sense of who she was and helped her explore her aptitudes and talents unbound by any expectations of who in the family she might take after. I tried not to squelch her natural feistiness knowing she would need it to deal with the White world. I put her in the public schools with the highest minority populations. We did things with other adoptive families that looked like ours. Today she is a strong, independent, intelligent, caring person, a loving wife and mother, and I am very proud of her. We have little in common, but we are bound by our shared history, shared values, mutual respect, and our love for each other.

My obituary will say I am survived by one daughter. I am nothing but grateful.

Pam Osborne has been an avid reader since 1st grade and carried that avocation into a career as a professional librarian. She facilitates women's groups, quilts, sings in a community choir, volunteers for hospice, and revels in her grandchildren. She writes personal essays and blogs about life at stirringswithin.com/blog.

"I was a willful child. That willfulness is not something that has gone away, though I like to think I've learned how to channel it."

- Temple Lentz

In 2018, 60% of voters in my district elected me to serve as their representative on the Clark County Council. It's become a cliché to say it, but serving in this position truly is an honor and a privilege. Something that gets said a little less often but is no less true, is that serving in this position is also a lot of work...at least, it's a lot of work to try to do it right. And I'm grateful to have the opportunity to do it. Before my election to office, I spent about a decade as an activist, advocate, and satirist of local government. I have become fully immersed in politics and fully engaged in trying to make a meaningful difference in an increasingly chaotic political world.

I recently visited my parents in the Midwest, where I grew up, and was reminded that my engagement in politics has not always been so strong.

I was a willful child. That willfulness is not something that has gone away, though I like to think I've learned how to channel it. But early on, it was complicated by an almost crippling shyness. I was terrified of people outside my immediate family. While this wasn't much of a problem for the first couple of years, and may even have been a little cute, it presented a bit of a hurdle for my working parents when they needed to send me to preschool.

Did I mention I was willful? Apparently, drop-off time at Montessori school elicited near-nuclear meltdowns that lasted for hours, well after my mom and dad were long out of view. I say "apparently," because I have no memory of this. When I asked my parents about it, however, they were immediately re-traumatized.

"I can still hear it," my mother said, sitting perfectly still and looking off into the distance. "You were so. Loud. So loud."

My father handed her a glass of bourbon and rubbed her shoulders. "There were at least three days I specifically remember thinking I'd leave you there and never come back," he said.

"We seriously considered it," my mother added. "But then we remembered, they had our address and phone number. There was no way we'd get away with it."

I come from a long line of white Protestants, flavored with a heaping tablespoon of German stoicism and just a *soupçon* of French *joie de vivre*. To this day, my father will laugh at Jerry Lewis but say it's undignified to smile when you're having your picture taken.

This translated into a rather uncomfortable emotional duality. From Montessori days onward, I was trained to believe it's OK to *have* strong emotions...it's just not OK to let anyone know about them.

Once my parents realized I wasn't going to stop my Montessori meltdowns, and that school management was preparing to cut me loose, they developed a new tactic. I was allowed to *feel* like crying, my mother said, but I needed to keep a lid on it and be strong because crying was private and undignified.

To be clear, like many three-year-olds in the '70s, I spent most of my days half-covered in jam. Dignity wasn't my strong suit. But I'd heard people say my grandmother was dignified, and I thought my grandmother was a perfect human, so I agreed to give the dignity thing a try.

And so, we negotiated. My mother, my father, and their new and improved dignified toddler bargained an agreement. If I was going to scream and cry and carry on, I must do it *before* getting to the door for dropoff. I could cry all I wanted in the car, but I had to stop once we arrived and be sniffle-free on entry.

This, they argued, would set a good example, demonstrate dignity, and respect the rights of others to come to school without wondering if someone was torturing the Lentz girl.

And so began a lifetime of feeling strong emotions, and finding complicated ways to express them.

Do high schools still have superlative contests? Those senior-year awards for "Most Likely to [Blank]," or "[Shallow Descriptor]-est Person?"

We had them in Delaware, Ohio, and in 1993 it was my class's turn. A month before graduation, we were instructed by our student body leadership that it was time for our final group activity: to reducing ourselves and our classmates to one-dimensional caricatures that would be printed on fancy paper and framed for posterity.

In high school, I was superlatively not superlative. I wasn't pretty and I wasn't ugly. I wasn't outgoing but I was no longer cripplingly shy. I was funny but not the funniest, smart but not the smartest.

And like most of my friends and colleagues in high school, by the end of Senior year I was ready to be done. For some, it was the end of their best years and the memories needed to be cherished. For others, we were on the cusp of beginning new, more interesting chapters. We had spent 12 years in compulsory education. If we were lucky, most of us had learned something and all of us had gained some experience. And we were ready to be free of being controlled and scheduled and told what to do and how to do it for all of those years.

The school I went to was large enough not to be cloying, but small enough that it was possible to know or at least be familiar with everyone in the graduating class. After spending what was, to us, a lifetime getting to know each other and learning about our classmates by sheer fact of proximity, the idea of boiling everyone down to something narrow, obvious, and probably somewhat inaccurate began to grate on me.

Sure, Dave was most likely to be a doctor, given that his father was the town doctor and he'd always been Pre-Med. But what if Dave got there and discovered

ered he loved art history and would really turn out to be a curator for a small contemporary art museum?

And yes, Sarah with her stunningly symmetrical features would clearly be named Prettiest Girl. But what if she was tired of being judged for her looks and wanted people to take her more seriously?

And then there was Misty, definitely the pick for Meanest Person. Everyone who met her knew she'd be doing hard time within 6 months of graduation, but was it really our job to enshrine that as the summation of all of her future prospects?

The more I thought about it, the more angrier I became about this manufactured end to our high school years. This wasn't just a popularity contest, it was an exercise in confirmation bias. We were better than this.

Screaming and crying about injustice were not options (see: Montessori School), so I decided to use the contest itself to demonstrate how ridiculous it was.

I decided to campaign for Meanest Person.

We all knew Misty was the front-runner, but I didn't think she'd mind the competition.

I'd never campaigned for anything before, but I'd seen the movie *Bob Roberts*, so I plowed ahead.

My campaign tagline was "Temple hates me but she hates you more."

With posterboard and markers, I made signs for the hallways. With colored pencil, paper, and scotch tape I made makeshift campaign buttons. I stalked through the halls slapping them onto people's chests and telling them they looked like shit today.

The "Most Likely Tos" were not something people had ever campaigned for, so there was no debate or talent show or opportunity to give a stump speech. Instead, I went around to every table in the cafeteria, gently shoved the person who would be least likely to hit me back, and told everyone at the table that they were ugly or stupid. Then I left a flyer on the table and scurried away.

At the end of two weeks, I was confident I had made my case. I'd identified my voters, delivered my message, and made personal contact. I'd bared my teeth and showed my resolve. I'd channeled my anger at the system that created the superlative contest and demonstrated my point that the whole thing was ridiculous.

And further, my chances to win were pretty good. The only campaigning Misty had done was to punch two girls in the bathroom and get suspended. While it was a bold move and strong campaign messaging, she hadn't even been at school for most of the last week because of the suspension! You can't take that much time off the campaign trail and expect to retain your lead. Victory was mine!

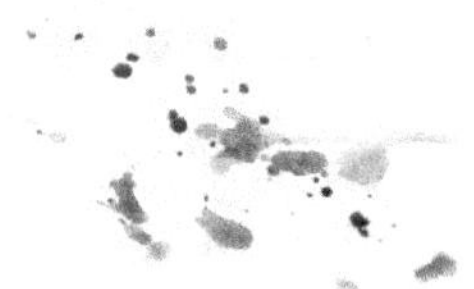

The day was finally upon us. Senior Day. Election Day. We would learn the results and I would claim my prize as Meanest Person of the Rutherford B. Hayes High School Class of 1993. I would save one soul from eternal ignominy and I would show that one person could indeed change the world. Or if not that, then one person could at least change the outcome of an archaic practice at a middle-of-the-road high school in small-town central Ohio.

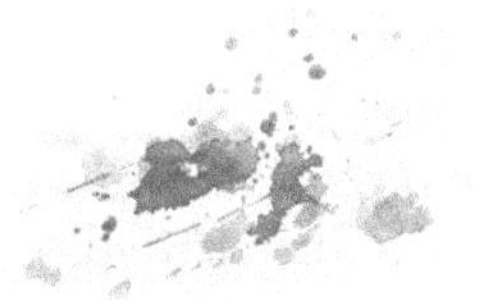

But it was all in vain. Misty won.

Not only did she win, she cleaned house. I barely registered as an also-ran.

And while I quivered with anticipation and then, slumped with defeat, Misty wasn't even there. Her probation officer said she was too volatile to be trusted in a group setting without more than one exit.

I was crushed. What had started as an experiment had become a passion. The emotion was strong, and it was about to overtake me. I felt my eyes well with tears, and I had to leave the room.

Two of my friends followed me into the bathroom and stood with me while I took deep breaths and blinked back tears. They assured me this was actually a good thing.

"Um, you're not actually mean," my friend Heidi said drily. "You said '"Sorry"' every time you pushed someone, and then you held the door for them. They voted for the person who's *actually* mean."

Eventually, I realized they were right. And as we now navigate the politics

of the early 21st Century, I suppose it's charming to be able to look back on a time when the electorate voted based on one's actual qualifications for office.

I've never been interested in politics so much as I am in people. What do people care about, think about, dream about? How can we help each other, and how can we move forward together? These are things that get me worked up today.

It wasn't until I moved to Vancouver, Washington, at age 30 that I finally understood how politics, especially local politics, can make a meaningful difference in the lives of real people. A lot of the job is mundane: road vacations, contract approvals, approval of minutes. But a lot of it matters in a very real way to the people I encounter every day on the street, in the grocery store, on local social media. As a community, we have the opportunity to talk, together, about who we want to be, where we want to go, and how we want to get there. As our world becomes more fractious every day, local politics is an opportunity to remember that we are all people, and most of us are doing the best we can with what we have.

My campaign approach these days has shifted from 1993, and I'm happy to be in a position where I can bring a different voice to the conversation and represent the perspectives of those who elected me. I remain willful, but the shape it's taken has changed a lot since the Montessori school parking lot.

Shortly after my crushing high school defeat at the Meanest Person polls, I stepped out of the bathroom with my friends and the celebration of superlatives was still going on. Our friend Steve from Drama Club was sweeping the Best Dressed, Best Dancer, and Best Hair categories.

As we watched him exit the stage, Heidi leaned over to me and said, "You're going to want to pay attention to this one."

There was one race left.

Apparently it was one I'd qualified for, and it was a landslide victory.

My classmates had named me Most Likely to Be a Politician.

Temple Lentz currently serves on the Clark County Council in Vancouver, Washington. Previously, she was a theatre professional, nonprofit leader, marketing consultant, and interpretive writer. She likes variety in job descriptions but the throughline of her work has always been writing and communication. She is a graduate of the University of Chicago and is slowly chipping away at a Master's degree. In Vancouver, she wrote the popular Daily 'Couve blog, a satirical look at local politics. She also created and hosted Hello Vancouver!, a live, local talk show. Believe it or not, she is also a hard Introvert with an Extrovert flex.

"At some point
I understood
that this journey
I was on was my
actual life."

Starve, Stress, Wallow

- Elizabeth Holmes

Remember in 2006 when everyone lost their minds over the book *Eat, Pray, Love: One Woman's Search for Everything Across Italy, India and Indonesia* by Elizabeth Gilbert? With its 187 weeks on the NY Times Best Seller list and its ubiquity across book clubs, you would have to have been asleep, or someone other than a middle-class white woman, at the time to sleep on that phenomenon. As a card-carrying member of the target audience, I felt like the book was a vitamin being shoved down my throat by well-meaning friends for the better part of 2006-2010. Instead of dying off after four years, the embers were fanned to a roaring flame by the release of a movie adaptation of the book starring the ever charming Julia Roberts and we were off again on a round of chatter about how the book changed lives.

If you weren't part of the demographic who was convinced it was their new bible and have no idea about *Eat, Pray, Love,* let me enlighten you. It's Liz Gilbert's memoir about her existential crisis at 34 and how she moved through it. She found herself stuck in a life and marriage she didn't want. She divorced her husband and then took separate trips to Italy, India and Indonesia, had adventures, learned about herself and fell in love, both with herself and a new man along the way. Sounds kind of delightful, right?

I resisted reading it for years. Having Oprah praise it didn't help, it intensified the efforts of my bookish friends to insist that I read it. I wasn't convinced. At that time, my life didn't allow for escapes to different continents or wild pivots that would upend my carefully curated routines. Why would I want to read about someone who did that? There was my demanding career that I was committed to advancing, two young kids to whom I was committed to being the very best mom, my marriage where I was committed to being the best wife in the land and then my various community board and commission roles that I was committed to being the absolute most valuable asset I could possibly be, that didn't leave a whole lot of time to commit to reading. Especially about a woman who, in my mind at the time, skipped out on all of her responsibilities to indulge in finding herself. Hard pass for me.

Around the time the film was released one of my world traveling relatives was visiting and mentioned that he loved the book and that it changed his life. Cue the record scratch. I didn't even know this guy read.

That was compelling.

So, I bought it but it still sat on my "to be read" pile for months. Eventually I did pick it up and start reading. It's a great book, I could see why it was well received, but, I did not enjoy that book.

Clearly, I'm in the minority. I get that and that's ok. It's cool.

As I mentioned, at that time I had an overfull plate of obligations that I was committed to performing perfectly and pleasing the imaginary panel of judges the would deem me "Best Woman Ever" or whatever I imagined the payoff was going to be for my efforts. I was all in on the life I was living. And, SPOILER ALERT the bulk of the book is Liz Gilbert running away from her life to glamorous and exotic locales to do her eating, her praying and her loving. As in, she had no ties that kept her place bound. It didn't even appear that she cared that much about the imaginary panel of judges and doing things perfectly. How in the world could I relate to that attitude?

I rage read it so I could put a check mark on another item on my list. I clucked away the whole time about how it must be nice to be able to pick up and leave. To have friends in exotic locales and to be a writer so it's actually your job to live that life and write about it. To say that I was living a different life from dear Liz at that moment was an understatement. The book did get me thinking – was I truly happy with the life I was building? Was there even space in life to pause and get perspective? The pace I was living at certainly didn't afford me that opportunity.

While I was reading about Liz jetting off to Italy to eat pasta and gelato and find a lover, I was cracking under the pressure of my own life. The only scene from the book that resonated with me was the one early on when she finds herself lying on her bathroom floor having a nervous breakdown. She feels trapped in a life that she was told she wanted versus creating a life her heart needed. That dark night of the soul spoke to me. The next steps to leave her husband and plan international travel, not so much.

I did end up leaving my career. Which felt like a kind of divorce. Having been raised with no safety net, I'd let my scarcity mindset convince me that I had to stay in a career that was sucking me dry in order to pay the bills. The idea of leaving made me shaky in my insides.

Once I made the decision to quit, instead of immersing myself in Italian culture and learning to appreciate and accept abandoned parts of my sensuality through food as Liz did in Italy, I entered a cycle with food that went something like this: I had an anxious stomach that was tied in knots all the time and food sounded disgusting so I didn't eat and that made my weight drop at an alarming rate, which flared my anxiety and looped me back to that tight stomach. I, being the rational being that I am, was convinced the weight loss was from some sort of undiagnosed eighteenth-century wasting disease. With the perspective of time, it seems more likely that the fact I thought twelve almonds was a pretty big lunch was behind the weight loss. My initial response to the burnout that was stalking me was to starve, not eat.

Having no career left me with a void where my identity had been. Raised by a working mom, I took my value from paid work. Leaving that behind revealed that my self esteem was built on a house of cards. Work friends stopped calling as their world went on without me. Mothering felt like a project I was trying to pick up in the middle. The routines I'd created with my kids revolved around meeting expectations. Organized and timely drop offs and pickups were the goal. I was training them to comply with what society expected. I started to pick up on how very wrong those lessons were. Everything I had counted on as being true and the right thing to do was called into question.

To add to the fun my body started speaking up and complaining loudly to let me know things were not ok. Trying to keep it together while experiencing crazy high levels of anxiety and rapidly diminishing physical mass wasn't working out. A wide spectrum of symptoms and conditions presented themselves to be dealt with. In Liz's story she heads to India to elevate her spiritual practice. To pray, as it were.

Me?

I headed to all of the doctor's offices to *stress*.

My quest to find answers from medical professionals kicked off. Similar to Liz's quest to find spiritual answers. But mine was not at an ashram in India and mine cost a lot in medical bills and peace of mind.

I started with my family doctor, my GP, and, while sympathetic, she had no answers but we did run a tragically failed experiment with me and anti-depressants. After that debacle, she sent me forth armed with a variety of specialist referrals. I sat in a lot of waiting rooms and recited my health history ad nauseum. I ended up with lots of tests, a few procedures, a couple diagnosis but no clear path forward to return me to my former state of being. And little did I know at the time, but returning to my former state of being wasn't even on the table.

The common suggestion that the medical professionals floated my way was that perhaps what I suffered from was a case of *bored housewife*. That felt weird because I'd been a housewife for less than six months and I certainly didn't feel bored. Terrified, anxious and veering toward hopelessness were all feelings I contained but none of those are even in the neighborhood of bored. I'd never been dismissed by a medical professional before. The shrug and suggestion that I'd probably have to get used to living like this was beyond frustrating. And the shame? Oh, the shame. Feeling like I was failing at all the aspects of my life I was trying to juggle, here was the truth that I couldn't even be a good patient. I was humbled by this failure.

From there I moved into the *wallow* phase of my journey. While Liz was doing love in Indonesia living it up with a local shaman and falling in love with a man with a sexy accent, I was reduced to calling it a great day if I was able to take my kids to school and pick them up without a panic attack.

My hypervigilance was at eleven. For example, one of the diagnosis that I did receive was that I had a heart irregularity and, thanks to Dr. Google, I became convinced that any flutter in my heart rate was my fate being visited upon me and my children would, like characters in a Disney movie, become motherless and have to raise themselves. Since one of my plethora of symptoms was heart palpitations, every day became a fun game of *Is This the Day My Heart Finally Gives Out or Nah?* And, fun fact, stressing out about heart palpitations can lead to more of them. Fantastic.

I'd lost thirty-five pounds. I looked like a lollipop with my big head and stick-like body. I had zero energy. I convinced myself, with help from the aforementioned Dr. Google and a variety of message boards, that I was dying of some heretofore unknown disease, or collection of diseases. I wasn't exactly sure which, but all the helpful people parked on the various message boards were happy to share about their own misery and assure me that I wasn't alone, they were also likely dying as the neglectful medical community looked on. I felt sure that all the specialists who had been unable to diagnose me would feel really bad when they found out I died. I didn't feel seen and I didn't feel heard, so I settled in to slowly fade out of existence. I was full of self-pity. I bathed in how frustrated I was, how sad it all was and how no one was rescuing me.

Instead of the third leg of this trip being like Liz's which set her on a new course in life, freer and full of possibilities, mine was playing out in my suburban living room and featured me spending my time wrapped in a big blanket trying to get warm (another symptom) and overseeing elementary school homework from the couch.

Finally fed up with what felt like half of a life, I arose from my fainting couch to circle back with my GP. I spread my handful of diagnosis before her like a pack of cards and asked if she had any thoughts. Western medicine saw each body system in a discreet silo and insisted groups of symptoms weren't related. Things were wrong, they agreed, but nothing was wrong enough to explain my cocktail of symptoms. I was losing my grip on my sanity.

My doctor made another half-hearted pass at getting me to try a different anti-depressant, which I declined. Of course I was depressed, my life had shrunk both literally and figuratively. My weight would have made a super model proud and my days consisted of school runs and, if I was lucky, a turn around the grocery store. Then the doctor mentioned that there were some studies that showed that thirty minutes of walking three times a week had the same effect as medication. First of all, this was infuriating because this seemed like information that should have been offered up front and second of all, I felt a glimmer of hope for the first time in over a year.

So, Dear Reader, do you know what I did? I started walking on the treadmill that had been sitting in my garage for more years than I care to admit for thirty minutes a day every day of the week. Days turned into weeks and I started to feel better. So slowly I was barely aware of it but I began to see that this routine allowed me to move up a rung on the ladder out of this cesspool. I started to feel like maybe I had it in me to climb up another.

A friend suggested I consult a naturopath. Great, I found a naturopath. The naturopath didn't seem puzzled by my array of symptoms in the slightest. She put me on an elimination diet and suggested I find an acupuncturist. Done. The acupuncturist I found also didn't blink at my list of issues and suggested I find a therapist. Which I did, and these protocols together helped me feel more in control of my life.

Then I went kind of crazy and consulted with all manner of alternative practitioners including, but not limited to, reiki masters, meditation, a shaman, an ayurvedic practitioner, a coven, an allergy specialist, an intuitive healer, and sound bathing. I left no stone unturned in my quest for healing. I believe Liz Gilbert would approve.

I shrugged off all I thought I knew about life and learned to be willing to move into a space that wasn't defined by rigid rules and double-blind studies but respected the systems of the body and the connection between the body and the mind. I had to have faith and listen to my gut. Sometimes literally. Those were things that had been worn away inside me by the friction of the relentless achievement lifestyle I'd chosen. To heal I had to connect with my kids and see them as the people that they are and take the medicine they were offering me. I had to release cynicism about finding a shaman in suburban Beaverton and instead sit with the healing she brought me.

Each experience helped me pull myself further from the depths. I refused to look down and, after a while, I stopped trying to gauge how much further I had to go. At some point I understood that this journey I was on was my actual life. Not a way to reach a predefined goal, but the process of living. I paused and looked around to see that everything was different. I was different.

My shit started to square up and I invested in my relationship with my kids in a new way. I dropped so many of the shoulds I'd lived with for so long. I read voraciously and expanded my knowledge. My marriage moved into a new phase where we are more than business partners managing a family together. I became less self-absorbed and more patient. My sense of humor came back. I accepted that my goal of getting back to where I was would never be met because I didn't want to go there, I wanted to see where this path led. It was infinitely more interesting. Then, the most exciting and transformative thing happened: I started to really love myself. And found that I'm perfect at being me.

If I read it again, I still don't think I'd enjoy *Eat Pray Love*, it reads like you have to leave what is familiar to experience life in a new way. The challenge truly is to find the unfamiliar in the familiar, to find the extraordinary in the ordinary and to believe in your capacity to heal yourself.

When it does come time to write my obituary, it could read pretty standard – birth, school, marriage, kids, career, a few accolades – but what would be omitted would be this horrible, amazing time that turned my life upside down and resulted in a better me than I ever imagined.

Elizabeth Holmes is a work in progress.

Her life has careened wildly from 90's grunge Superfan to respectable career woman to stay at home mom to the latest chapter which is uncharted. She's finding that both exhilarating and terrifying. She's at work on a novel and her musings are available at radiantbadass.com.

"I had to begin the process of figuring out how to screw up royally and still live a life."

Omitted

- Alissa Fencsik

She loved her family and her friends and her church. She enjoyed reading and movies, and retained a terrifying amount of celebrity trivia in her head, often at the expense of other important memories from her actual life. She tried to do the right thing all the time and lived in mortal terror of doing something that would disappoint people, and then she did. She really did. She disappointed everyone who mattered to her, and lived for quite a few years after that, to her great surprise.

I've never wanted to disappoint anyone. As a child, I lost a ring my parents had given me, and thus began my lifelong relationship with panic attacks as I struggled to hide a relatively minor mistake. In school, I got good grades and engaged in afterschool activities, fighting against my natural inclination to procrastinate in order to keep my teachers happy. As a teenager, I conducted my adolescent rebellion as an exchange student in Brazil, lest my parents endure the sight of, you know, the stuff pretty much all teens do. As an adult, I've done my best to volunteer, to show up, to get it done, to follow the rules, to wait my turn, to meet the need, to be a functional, contributing member of society.

"People Pleaser" is such a benign phrase. I picture a 1950s-era housewife, sporting a frilly apron and passing a tray of hors d'oeuvres with one hand while vacuuming with the other. Women talk about this trait, this habit, this...mania - like it's a quirk of being female. We talk about how tiring it is to manage and meet other people's expectations. It's a sort of marathon where we're both running and passing out the cups of water. But it's even more insidious than that sort of unrelenting correctness. Because so many of us believe that if we can't do or be the right thing every moment in a way that is deeply pleasing to those we love and those we like or respect, we have failed. The margin of error is zero.

So when your error is big, like - say- a DUI on the way home from work that results in a night in jail and a year of previously unexperienced engagement with the legal system and its many costs of all kinds, you might feel singularly unprepared for that first wave of shame that crashes over you, leaving you gasping in the sand until the next one comes.

This isn't a Getting Sober story. Those stories are important and necessary, but mine isn't interesting. I just stopped. The arrest served as the short, sharp shock Buddhists talk about that reorients your thinking, and I reset my habits immediately. It's not even a Falling Down and Getting Up story. Those are inspiring, but the work I needed to do was different. It was about listening, observing, and letting myself see and understand what happens when the sort of Worst Thing your neurotic imagination has been conjuring actually happens.

Of course, there was some action on my part, and consequences. I gave up alcohol except for my weekly hit of Communion wine and the occasional sip of my husband's beer, if it's a really good one. Once I'd had time to process what had happened, I told some people, like my family and my close friends, and eventually my employer. I apologized to my husband and my children, repeatedly and sincerely, and listened to what they had to say about how they felt about what I had done. I attended the mandatory DUI alcohol education class and the MADD victim impact panel. I spent a month without driving, and another several with a breathalyzer installed in my car. I paid fines and fees in court and attorney fees and course fees and installation fees, totaling thousands of dollars, so we can also add to my personal suckage ledger the undermining of my family's financial health.

Please understand: I DESERVED THIS. All of it. I did a very wrong thing, knowing it was wrong and endangering other people and myself, and by extension my family. I can "yes but" with the best of them, but I broke the law. And I know that for some people, especially those who have lost someone they love to the carelessness of a driver like me, this bad choice is beyond the pale, and they're right. I own that.

So what next? Even in the midst of letting the wheels of justice turn (slowly) and doing the things I had to do to comply with my sentence and my situation, I had to begin the process of figuring out how to screw up royally and still live a life. What if you demonstrate in some concrete way that you are not the person your loved ones thought you were? What if all the rule-following and needs-meeting and turn-waiting suddenly seems like a persona you've been hiding behind, while your real self – the one who is lost and confused and frankly dumb much of the time – is revealed in stark white light? My husband has known me for two and a half decades, and I guarantee you he's never labored under the illusion that I'm perfect, but it's a real leap from I-can't-find-the-checkbook to can-you-pick-me-up-from-jail? Obviously, my kids have known me for their whole lives, but how do they reconcile She Who Must Be Obeyed with She Who Did Something Way Worse Than I Ever Have?

From my perspective, their process of dealing with it looked like anger, sadness, worry, compassion and even a sort of nonchalant shrug from the youngest, who didn't really think it was a big deal until waiting for the car breathalyzer to warm up in the morning almost led to school tardiness. But here's the thing: I had to sit back and let them feel however they were going to feel. I couldn't move them along to feel about me the way I wanted them to feel. I couldn't explain or justify or apologize their feelings in a new direction that felt more comfortable to me. I had disappointed them, and as I had feared since the beginning of time, I just had to sit with it, whatever "it" looked like. I realized that this obsession with pleasing people is a way of stage managing their reaction to me, and it took me really failing to please anyone to understand that. I had to show them that I heard them by making changes, so I did.

A fun thing over which you also have no control is that the original screw-up can spiral out in unexpected ways, and even your attempts to fix it can lead to new and different forms of letting people down. I lost a close friend because I wasn't drinking anymore. She was deeply supportive during the acute phase, agreeing that the DUI may have been a gift because she had been concerned that my drinking was out of hand, and I've truly never felt judged by her for my mistake. But as the incident gets smaller and smaller in my rearview mirror, so to speak, so does she. I'm not the wine-swilling, day-drinking fun friend I used to be. My volume is lower, my hilarity more subdued. We're in different places, and I just have to sip my mineral water and accept it. My current incarnation isn't wrong, but it is different, and there are consequences to that too.

With the exception of the occasional viral obituary from a family who have clearly been holding their collective breath until a real jackass of a relative dies so they can let loose with every grievance, you rarely see a person's rap sheet come up. I'm pretty sure I've engendered enough goodwill that my family will keep this one gnarly incident to themselves and I'll get the usual rundown of hobbies and accomplishments. That said, I'm inclined to think I wouldn't mind. We all make mistakes, but we're all worthy of love, and forgiveness, and the latitude to learn from our own worst selves. If I'd known years ago that it was possible to make an enormous error, acknowledge it, take the lesson, and move the hell on, I'd have been looser, less anxious, and taken a few more leaps. Preferably not the stupid kind that end with a chauffeured ride in a cop car, but the brave kind of mistakes that can result in tighter connections with my loved ones and a renewed sense of my own value in the world.

Alissa Fencsik is a writer, reader, specialist in operations management, church lady, and an obsessive chronicler of the lives of her pets. After stints in Portland, Ann Arbor, and Boston, during which she worked for the late lamented Borders Books and then as a non-profit consultant, she now lives in the Bay Area with her family.

"All the while I was using my words to serve the much deeper purpose of keeping me alive"

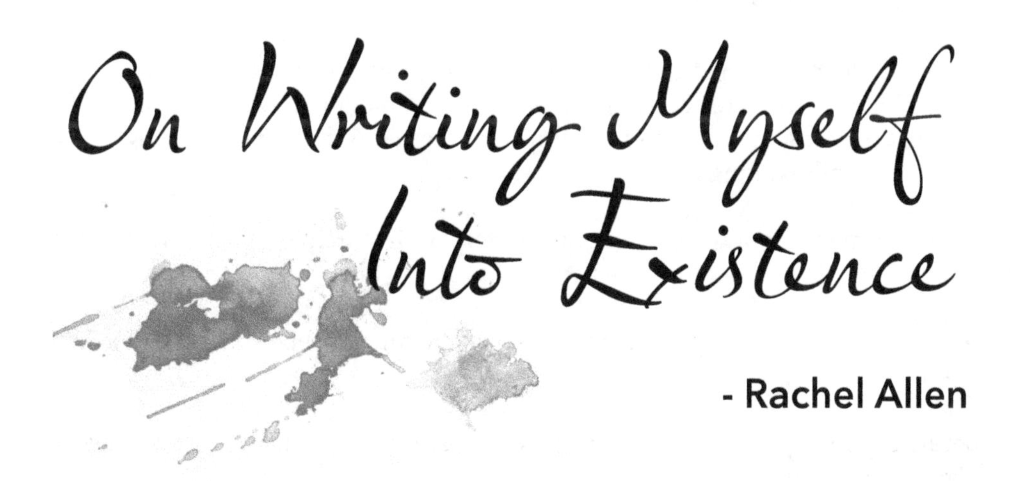

On Writing Myself Into Existence

- Rachel Allen

Anyone who's grown up in a truly small town knows you have a couple very specific options for getting out:

Fighting, fucking, sports, or smarts.

You can join the military.

You can marry someone from somewhere else.

You can get out on a sports scholarship and bash your head in playing college football.

Or you can be smart enough to go to college, ideally out of state, although that of course costs more; the trade of dollars for miles is worth it to many though.

It certainly was to me.

Smarts was my avenue, being strikingly un-nationalistic, not pretty enough or savvy enough to manufacture some wiles to snare an out-of-towner, and absolutely no good at sports.

What I *am* good at is learning a whole bunch of information really fast, and then writing about it in a way that serves a purpose.

In the beginning, my purpose was to get A's, because the equation I was sold on was A's = a college out of state = a good job = a home where there's food and running water all of the time, instead of just some of it.

When, in 2008, it turned out that this equation was a lie for me, I turned that same skill of writing to serve a purpose towards making a living, starting with freelance writing and going on to build an international agency that regularly runs a 6 month waiting list.

All that time though, I had a secret mission, an instinctive, raw grasping that I'm only now coming to understand.

All the while I was using my words to serve the much deeper purpose of keeping me alive.

Because, you see, there's one more way to leave small towns that people don't like to talk about: suicide.

I was standing on the worn carpet outside the Calculus classroom in my high school, messing with the dropped hem on my tic-tac-toe-graffitied plaid skirt. Shoulders aching from a backpack filled with college textbooks and designed before ergonomics were a thing.

My day, up until 5 minutes before, had been going OK. Pretty well, in fact, by my standards. I'd got a solid 3 hours of sleep, had gotten good feedback on my analysis of the questions of postmodern identity in Virginia Woolf's *To the Lighthouse,* and it had been Chick-fil-a day in the cafeteria.

Then she told me.

"Your mother told me yesterday that everything in your family would be perfect if it wasn't for you."

A friend of the family, sympathetic to me, had only had a minute to tell me in passing. Looking back now, I think she was warning me.

In the full body cold, numb that settled on me, everything got very clear. My body felt the surge of sorrow as my stomach dropped in shame. My mind went into hyper-analysis, assessing that I had about 90 seconds before the next period started, big emotions were dangerous, and besides, it's not like I could be all that surprised. People don't love those they call ugly hags, lying bitches, unlovable witches.

Logically, I knew this.

So, very methodically, I shut it down. The physical sensations. The tears that tightened my sinuses and closed my throat. The voice of outraged despair that said, "But they're my parents, they *should* love me."

I didn't have time for should.

I had time for survival.

So I survived. With a drive that I understand comes from biological need, but am still ashamed of, I tried everything I could to make my parents love me, or at least tolerate me. There's a reason monkeys would rather cling to an electric facsimile of a mother monkey that shocks them, rather than abandon the mother altogether. They do everything they can think of to appease it, taking the pain in hopes that one day, it will become a real mother and stop hurting them.

My version of that was trying on different personalities, writing new parts for myself, hoping that I'd hit on one that would make my hag-faced, bitchy, unlovable self more palatable.

I was the obedient Christian daughter.

I was the rebel who didn't even care, because she didn't even need a family anyway.

I was the smartest girl in class.

I was the dumb girl who was easy to be around because she was so dependent on her smarter father to help her with her homework. Never mind that I'd actually finished it myself days before. The boredom of repetition beats rejection any day.

I was by turns good and bad, smart and dumb, and everything else I could think of.

My characterizations were perfect. I became a shockingly good observer of details and body language. I wrote my new parts right down to the details of tone of voice and clothing choice.

When nothing took, after months and months of failed personae, I eventually realized that there was one fundamental commonality among them: me.

There was something about me so bad, so broken, so wrong that even my own parents couldn't stand the sight of me — any of the me's!

So I started looking hard at that final option for escape.

I grew up on farms, I understand the importance of getting rid of bad stock, and I understand putting animals out of their misery.

So I picked that option up every now and again, like an old friend, adding my own injuries to the tapestry already on my body.

I never quite followed all the way through on it.

I still don't entirely know why.

But I do strongly suspect a big part of it was because one of my many personalities had been a surprise hit with another audience — classy, quiet, cultured Rachel was playing very well with the family of one of my friends.

It's quite a thing for a girl who comes from a steady diet of mac and cheese and pre-frozen ground beef, and all the sugar she can fit in her body, best served with cutlery gripped cave-man-style and a conversational flow that consisted largely of grunts from her father and brother to get dropped into the middle of a dinner where there were seating arrangements! Flowers on the table! Multiple forks and wine glasses!

I studied for weeks before the dinner, drawing — and for some reason, hand-calligraphy-ing — a place mat for myself with outlines of all the bits and pieces of a fancy place setting.

I practiced at dinner, choosing my imaginary salad fork for my "first course" of mashed potatoes, then following up with the bigger fork for my main dish of a rubbery pork chop, delicately cutting the thick layer of fat off, being sure to hold my fork in my left and my knife in my right, like Europeans do.

When ice cream came later, I imagined my beat-up tablespoon was a demitasse spoon, and wondered if it was pronounced "demi-tas" or "demi-tassi".

When the day of the dinner finally came, I was terrified. I watched and imitated my hosts religiously. I brought out my best conversation (and had bullet points on an index card I could look at if I ran to the bathroom with my purse.) I listened with what must have been an alarming degree of intensity, figuring out how to fit into the flow of conversation and agreeing with everyone else's opinions. The woman on my left liked CS Lewis? I liked CS Lewis! The man across from me wasn't a fan of the latest shift in financial laws that impacted his taxes? I was totally with him. (Even though I couldn't have told you beans about anyone's actual tax situation.)

And when the dinner was over, and I overheard a woman saying "That girl has beautiful manners!" I felt a flash of something so unfamiliar in my solar plexus it took me a minute to recognize it.

Happiness.

That dinner, and the ones that followed were, looking back now, gatherings of medium-sized fish in a very small pond.

To me at the time though, they were the famed salons of the Belle Epoque. They were the fast-paced high-class parties of the as-of-yet-mythical-to-me New York. They were the delightfully genteel gatherings of the literati, not a casual dinner party of local doctors, lawyers, and that one couple that owned the gas station that had a nice deli.

Regardless, they opened up my mind to a different way of thinking about life. One where things were altogether grander in scale.

On good days, I thought I might be able to one day join that life myself. Hop the tracks from the family tradition of getting married, moving in near my mother, having kids, and slowly going crazy as they grew up and stopped needing me.

On bad days, those tracks seemed so far out of my realm of possibility I might have dreamed them.

And I was *so* tired.

Physically.
Emotionally.
Mentally.

So as appealing as Quietly Cultured Rachel and her dream life was, White Trash Rachel and her very-much-not-a-dream reality got more airtime.

I never seriously harmed my body. Little cuts here and there. Bruises, some deeper than others. Burns, and pinches. The occasional pin shoved in the flesh of my arm.

But I did commit a sort of suicide of the self.

With the knowledge of how bad, how wrong I was, reinforced by constant messaging that I was crazy, that I couldn't trust my perceptions of reality, that those good things that happened to me didn't really happen, and those people who said they liked me and enjoyed my company were just lying to me because they knew how crazy I was and were scared they'd set me off...

I abandoned myself.

I deadened my desires.

I relinquished my right to a grip on reality, only ever half-sure that what I was seeing and hearing and feeling was real.

I decided I couldn't trust myself, that I couldn't even trust the basic physical messages of my body, like "hungry" or "pain".

I went to college a year or so later. Slept most of the time. Rode panic attack after panic attack the rest of the time.

The second year I drank, and fell in love with a very Romantic anarchist who broke my heart (and was a trifling 16 years older than me, 35 to my 19.)

Reeling from it, I used my third year to run away. I moved to Hong Kong, and promptly fell in love again. This time with a crazy-smart philosopher who took me on an all night date to a karaoke bar, then held my hand as we took the sunrise ferry from Wan Chai back to his place.

He really liked Quietly Cultured Rachel. She was so smart, so classy, so easy to get along with. She never said no to anything, always went where he wanted to go, watched what he wanted to watch, didn't say boo when he showed up 20, 30, 50 minutes late to pick her up.

We moved in together the day after our first date, and adventured for 9 years.

Something else happened around that same time I met the philosopher though.

I graduated college, and the 2008 job market hit me like a ton of very expensive bricks of wasted potential.

My triple-major degree and gold-plated internship got me a job unpacking boxes in the Old Navy warehouse.

And, surrounded by my fellow underemployed liberal arts majors, something popped in my brain.

An act of will.

The realization, like waking from a dream, that *this was not what I wanted.*

I didn't know what I *did* want. But I knew it wasn't this. And, for the first time in years, I was ready to actually act on one of my own desires.

So the philosopher and I packed up and moved back to Hong Kong. I started the freelancing that led me to the here and now.

But — perhaps even more importantly — I started rewriting myself again. I started wondering if Quietly Cultured Rachel was all there was.

I started coming across stories from other people that helped me put words like "abuse" and "trauma" and "gaslighting" to my experience.

Kept writing.

Now the iterations came ever-faster.

Quietly Cultured Digital Nomad Rachel.

Quietly Cultured Digital Nomad Business Owner Rachel.

Not-So-Quiet-Anymore Cultured Digital Nomad Business Owner Rachel who knew for sure when she was in pain. Who began to slowly trust her own physical sensations again. Who laid the first bricks of rebuilding her surety of her grasp on reality.

Rachel who has healthily cut herself off from her family.

Rachel who, actually, doesn't like it when her live-in lover the philosopher is 20,

30, 50 minutes late to pick her up, doesn't actually enjoy Bach's Partitas and arthouse cinema to the degree he does. Rachel who *really* doesn't like it when they start fighting, and the fights get progressively uglier for three years.

Rachel who leaves because she can no longer allow anyone to abuse her, including herself, and staying in the situation she and the philosopher co-created would be abuse.

Rachel who has something to say about words and why they matter.

Rachel who's talking to you here today.

Draft, draft, draft.

Iteration, iteration, iteration.

I have written myself into existence.

That's how I know in every single reconstructed, reconnected, redeemed cell of my body the power of words.

Of reclaiming your narrative, being the one who writes your story.

Deciding who you are, and what you have to say.

And how innate this power is to every single human, even when we are at our most dehumanized.

You might not need to rewrite yourself into existence.

You do have *something* to say though. (We all do.)

It's my deepest wish that you will.

Rachel Allen is the owner of Bolt from the Blue Copywriting, where she and her team help businesses on a mission to use words to make money. By mixing the neuroscience of communication with the art of great writing, she creates the words and strategies that make it possible for businesses to take the cap off their income, impact, and influence. Ultimately, all her work is in service of one simple mission: to build the words that bring great ideas into reality, so they can have a tangible impact and move the global conversation forward.

www.boltfromthebluecopywriting.com
www.facebook.com/boltfromthebluecopywriting
www.instagram.com/boltfromthebluecopywriting

"I wanted people
to know my
situation was
special,
just like my
child."

- Kelliann Amico

It was pretty annoying being stuck behind the school bus. It was going below the speed limit, and the fumes were ghastly. The kids in the back of the bus were jumping around so much it made me dizzy. All the excitement of a field trip was packed into that giant yellow sardine can. I had so much work waiting for me in my home office, but here I was… trailing a school bus. An unwitting helicopter mom.

Today's journey behind the bus led back to that first fateful field trip the summer before kindergarten. Back then, the only reason my son, Milo, even attended "school" was so I could work. That Pre-K summer field trip to Oaks Park, I had reasoned, would make it worthwhile for my only child to go to school during the blessed summer months. It would give him the chance to flee my apron strings, be social, and play with kids his age. I was so excited - I just knew Milo was going to chatter about Oaks Park for days afterward. Although, it was admittedly a little disconcerting when I waved goodbye to him after the bus bound for the park had loaded, moments before it took off. Crocodile tears were raining from Milo's sweet little face, squished up against the window glass. Once he arrived, I justified, he'd forget his fear of the unknown and exchange it for sheer glee.

The call came about 40 minutes later while I was in a client meeting. Milo hadn't stopped crying. He was inconsolable. I made my apologies, left the meeting and beelined for Southeast Portland. Immediately upon entering that tired little amusement park I saw my tear-stained son. Then, he saw me, his face lit up and he came running toward me. I swept him into my arms and he cooed with relief. I spent the next two hours as a field trip chaperone, giggling alongside Milo on the rides, sharing cotton candy and succumbing to the joy of that sunny summer day. I could make money tomorrow.

After that, every time a notice came home regarding an upcoming field trip, I cleared my day and signed up as a chaperone. Nevermind that parents typically had to take turns volunteering to chaperone. My situation was special, just like my child. And unless there was a shortage of space, I was usually invited to take the school bus on field trips. So, I was taken aback when Milo's 4th grade teacher insisted I drive behind the school bus on this particular day. She expressed concern that Milo would have some kind of meltdown that would require the school bus to stop, that all of its passengers would be captive to his outburst, and the day would be ruined. Honestly, I told her, I had been on every field trip in Milo's school career and nothing of the sort had ever happened. She said my choice was clear: take Milo to the field trip destination in our family car, or drive behind the bus with Milo in the bus. Like hell was I going to separate Milo from his peers.

Once the 1-hour drive to the Bonneville Fish Hatchery was finished, I questioned why I even bothered to make Milo go on this field trip. He didn't want to go in the first place. We had just weeks before visited the same site together as a family. This was a new school for Milo, he didn't have any friends there, and it was just he and I wandering around seeing very familiar sights among a bunch of unruly kids. Milo ended up riding home with me in the car that day instead of returning in the school bus. On the way back to Portland, he confessed that he hated school buses for how noisy they are, and really didn't care if he ever rode one again, field trip or no. Lesson learned.

Diagnosis and trials

It became clear in preschool that Milo was atypical. While there wasn't a single telltale signal that we recognized - we were new parents, after all - we did perceive that our sweet Milo was a little bit different than the average kid. Perfect, but different. While not yet confirmed prior to the Pre-K field trip, it was old news by the 4th grade outing. Milo had autism. He still has it, but it's different now.

I suspected Asperger's syndrome when he was three but after a series of tests, Milo was dismissed by the developmental pediatrician with a shrug, and "I'm sorry, but I don't have any answers for you." But once Milo was in 2nd grade he was technically old enough to test again. That time, before my husband and I could even sit down, the newer and more savvy model of developmental pediatrician confirmed a diagnosis of Asperger's and ADHD. Within a year, the psychiatric bible known as DSM-5 replaced autistic disorder, Asperger's and other developmental disorders with the umbrella diagnosis of autism spectrum disorder. Asperger's had previously been interpreted by many as "a dash of autism" while autism as a diagnosis was a full mark.

I spent the next year or so being a bit secretive about the diagnosis. The stigma of it all. But over time, I began sharing the details with anyone who would listen. In my newfound awareness of Asperger's – technically autism – I wanted to help make others aware. Temple Grandin and, before that, her mom, nailed it in declaring that autism makes a person "different, but not less." I wanted people to know that about my son.

As for the ADHD part of the diagnosis, apparently autism is one of those disorders typically accompanied by a comorbidity – an equally challenging developmental difference that requires its own treatment protocol, and which sometimes exacerbates autism. So, when Milo's 4th grade teacher called to report that a child in Milo's class had been ruining other children's artwork by throwing tennis balls, books and scissors in the classroom, requiring all of the room's inhabitants to evacuate, it came as no surprise that the child she was speaking of was Milo. (Hence, the field trip school bus debacle.) Autism alone can make a person feel overwhelmed by sensory overload, uncomfortable social situations, and a break in routine, among other triggers. Throw in ADHD and the fight-or-flight instinct manifests as impulsivity.

My husband and I had never wanted to medicate our child, but Milo's school experience had become demoralizing by 4th grade. Over the years, we followed the lead of a string of developmental pediatricians, and tried several medications with varying degrees of success. It turns out anxiety is a huge byproduct of autism, and most attention medications are uppers, which intensify anxiety. Milo became a cranky and sleepless shell of himself.

Concerned by what I saw in Milo, I tried one of his uppers for myself. Within a half hour I felt as if I had consumed two quadruple espressos in rapid succession, becoming a machine in full throttle. As a spokesperson for one of my clients, I ended up being interviewed, impromptu, by KOPB that day. Yikes. I was an imposter, rattling off all kinds of data and talking points. I felt impressive in the moment, but was out of my body and overly anxious. Plus, the back of my neck got very stiff, I was grinding my teeth all day, and I had acid reflux. I couldn't eat a thing.

After my personal trial with the ADHD drug, we cut Milo's dose in half and limited the medication to school days only. It was strictly a school tool. But by the middle of 7th grade, we took our depressed son off the attention medication altogether. His teachers were blown away by his transformation. He was so engaging and kind, funny even. And they didn't notice any change in the amount of work he was able to complete, or not complete. Another lesson learned.

School, another school, more schools

No where else did Milo's differences reveal themselves than in the school setting, where Milo has been rejected and accepted in equal measure by school administrators and teachers over the years. When Milo was a toddler, our family of three, along with our dog, moved to a neighborhood in a desirable school district. Oddly enough, when we sought to transfer Milo to the neighborhood school in 3rd grade from the focus option program he'd been attending from kindergarten through 2nd grade, the neighborhood school principal made it abundantly clear that Milo was not welcome there.

Though the law was on our side in the unexpected neighborhood school predicament, this was not a battle we were interested in waging. It was just another in a string of rejections that included public schools in which Milo was

was enrolled, and private (and in this case, public) elementary and middle schools which refused to accept him as a student on the basis that they had their quota of kids on the spectrum, or didn't have the capacity to serve him. The administrator of one private school that was specifically designed for kids with autism and ADHD went so far to say that Milo just didn't fit into that school environment. The very same administrator moved on to another similar school the following year, and he rejected Milo's application for that school, too. So, it was public school or bust.

By November of 4th grade, about a month after that field trip, Milo was placed in a communication behavior classroom, where he remained through the end of 5th grade. Where he recited the days of the week on a daily basis with his peers in the classroom. Where he was enclosed in a classroom behind a baby gate for all other students in the school to see. Where he did the same level of math in 5th grade that he mastered in 1st grade. Where, were it not for the beautiful art projects he created in that timeframe, he wasted two years of his life. We commuted across town, 25 minutes each way, to bring him to this classroom. The kind teacher taught to the lower-functioning kids so everyone could be engaged. It was confusing for Milo, whose intelligence quotient easily surpasses mine, and utterly boring.

By the time Milo started at our neighborhood middle school, he had been through the doors of four preschools and three elementary schools.

Preschool #1 - "I'm sorry, but he's a loner and just doesn't fit in."

Preschool #2 - "He's too disruptive in the classroom, and threatens the sanctity of our learning environment."

Preschool #3 - "I love having Milo in my classroom. Please be assured that Milo's behaviors are not a reflection of your parenting. Whatever is going on with him is organic."

Preschool #4 - "You might consider having Milo seen by an occupational therapist and developmental pediatrician."

Kindergarten - "Milo is a puzzle and I'm really enjoying figuring out all his pieces."

1st grade - "Milo is intellectually gifted."

2nd grade - "Milo needs to figure out how to fit in."

3rd grade classroom #1 - "Milo is not the kind of learner who will thrive in our program."

3rd grade classroom #2 - "Milo is having a difficult time transitioning at his new school."

4th grade - "Milo is out of control."

5th grade - "Milo is artistic."

6th grade - "Milo has some behaviors we need to help him manage, but he'll be just fine. He's a great kid."

IEP armour

Throughout the school journey we tooled and retooled, then perfected some more, Milo's Individualized Education Program (IEP). The first draft, in kindergarten, was woo woo conceptual. But by 3rd grade we had hired our special education attorney, Diane Wiscarson. She saw to it that Milo was afforded every accommodation he needed, that every goal within his IEP was measurable, and that nothing was left to chance. She remains by our side today. I don't even want to imagine how difficult Milo's school years would have been to this point without her counsel and advocacy.

High school is where the bar has been raised. A few weeks into 9th grade, Milo was flunking every class. Overwhelmed with how to support Milo during this final stanza of public education, in which grades actually matter, I asked Milo's caseworker/home room teacher for suggestions. He offered to put Milo on the track for a modified diploma. Not an option. Then a couple of months later, after Milo's grades had improved, he suggested it again. I made it clear we were not going to have that conversation again and reminded him that because Milo has an IEP, he has until he's 21 to graduate from high school. I said I'd be more than happy for Milo to just take a couple classes per semester, if that's what he needs in order to remain on the regular diploma track. So, with one minor adjustment to his IEP, Milo is now in his second semester of 9th grade, and instead of taking eight classes, he's taking six. So far, he has all As and one B.

The open road

So, on this winding journey we continue. While tempting to laud light at the end of the tunnel, it isn't there just yet. But we'll get there. Milo will graduate, go to college (he really wants to), and achieve his dreams of starting an animal rescue and running Green Whiskers, our family's mobile dog grooming business that we, my husband in particular, launched in October 2018 for Milo to eventually take over.

I know that one day, in the not too distant future, I'll be driving behind a school bus just like the one I trailed when Milo was in 4th grade. And, I'll look in the rearview mirror at the back middle seat where Milo sat on the way to his first day of kindergarten... where he giddily exclaimed with a big beaming smile, "I'm excited to learn!" And, I'll remember it all, this journey. And, I'll know I will have done everything in my power to make sure Milo is prepared for the ride.

Kelliann Amico always wanted to be a mom. But having come of age in the early 80s, in the final rally of the "women's lib" movement, her career took center stage. Eager to climb that corporate ladder, she had her first PR job six months before graduating from the University of Portland in May 1986.

After more than a decade of working for some of the most respected public relations and public affairs firms in the Pacific Northwest, Kelliann started Amico Public Relations. She was immediately swept up by the Clinton White House as a press advance lead, and for the next few years traveled the world anywhere from one to three weeks in advance of Presidential and First Lady visits. She later worked for the Gore, Kerry and Hillary presidential campaigns, and also borrowed on her advance experience to manage press logistics for the Dalai Lama Environmental Summit in Portland, Oregon, in 2013.

Kelliann cultivated her client roster while jet setting for politicians, and has been honored over the years to represent a variety of organizations in a number of different industries. Her disciplines include earned media, media training, crisis communication, issues management and special events.

Kelliann met her husband in the fall of her freshman year of college, though it took 20 years before their first date. Four years later, in 2005, they welcomed their son, Milo, into this world. Charmed by a fulfilling career, being mom to Milo has proven to be Kelliann's best gig ever.

"I can now be thankful for what I've been through — I'm stronger because of it."

Finding Peace in Vulnerability

- Tayzsia Keohokalole

I used to walk through life afraid.

Every man was a potential threat, someone who could easily rob me of my peace.

I had a hard time engaging with the opposite sex, and resigned myself to the fact that I would never marry, or have children, even though having a family of my own was what I desired most in this life.

I didn't want to be like this. I didn't want the kind of life you survived, instead of lived. But it had been forced on me by three men when they decided to sexually assault me. I walked around half my life paralyzed by their choices. Now I'm thankful — not that it happened, but for what I've chosen to do with it. Here's how I got there.

The first time it happened, I was eight years old. My mom was addicted to crystal meth at the time, and had left my younger sister and I at a friend's house. This was nothing new... we were both used to her middle-of-the-night escapades. Before she left, my mother ushered my little sister and I to an empty bedroom to sleep in. Instead of falling asleep, we lay awake staring up at the ceiling, hoping our mom would come back soon.

After about an hour, a man appeared in the doorway. He doesn't do anything, he just ... stares. It felt like forever, but must have only been a minute or two. It still felt creepy, though. I try to rationalize it. I thought, "Maybe he just wants to check on us. He probably just wants to make sure we're OK." But that just didn't sit right.

30 minutes later, he was back. My sister was fast asleep by that time, so I was the only one who saw the man quietly place a chair in the doorway. He slowly sits down in it, and stares at us once more. He doesn't seem to realize that I am still awake, so I lay really still. I can feel my heart racing in my chest, wishing he'd just go away, wishing that my mother would return. I move my eyes to glance over at my sister; she's still fast asleep, her chest slowly rising and falling. I can't decide whether it's a good thing that she's asleep, and possibly safe, or a bad thing that she's not awake, to see this man's intentions.

Then I look up.

The man and I lock eyes.

My body freezes, thoughts race through my mind. I have no idea what to do.

He motions for me to come over to him.

"What could he possibly want from me?" I think to myself. I try to tell myself that maybe, he's going to tell me when my mother's coming back, and he needs me to come closer to him so we won't wake up my sister by talking.

Slowly, I get up and drag myself over to where he sits in his chair. He pulls me onto his lap and starts rubbing my back.

"Let me help you fall asleep," he breathes, in a voice that smells like cigarettes and beer.

"Where is my mother?" I ask in a squeaky, shaky voice. He doesn't reply. I try to get up, to twist my body away from him, but he doesn't let me go.

"Just relax," he says, stroking my thigh. His hand brushes higher and higher, and my heart beats faster and faster until I feel like my chest is going to burst open.

I keep praying for my mother to walk through the door. She doesn't.

I didn't tell my mother about that night until years later. There was no point in telling a drug addict anything, I reasoned. I was afraid to tell her, though. Afraid she wouldn't believe me. Afraid she would blame me. I resented her for what had happened to me, though, silently blaming her for that night.

Even though she didn't know why I was carrying that kind of feeling towards her, it put even more tension and strain on our already-complicated relationship. It was only after years of work on both our parts, and on that of my sister, that my mother and I were eventually able to have any kind of relationship at all. But even then, there were things we found really difficult to reconcile, including what happened next.

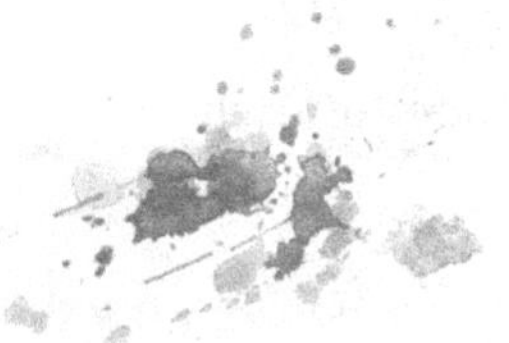

Years go by after that first encounter, and a couple of big things happen. Child Protective Services had removed my sister and I from my mother's custody on my 13th birthday, and placed us into our aunt's care. While at the time it felt like my world was falling apart, I now like to think of it as the best birthday gift I've ever been given. It turns out to be a strong motivator for my mother too, who, by the time I turned 16, had quit doing drugs and had a stable job.

To celebrate, we decided to go on a family camping trip. And to make it even better, we got to go with my favorite uncle, a trusted family member I adored and respected. We'd been close since before I was born — he and my aunt had taken my mother in after my grandmother kicked her out when she found out my mother was pregnant with me.

He spoiled me so much, even to the point of making me a totally different meal than the rest of the family, if I didn't want to eat what had already been made and wanted to eat something different. We had tickle wars, where he'd end up winning by tickling me till I cried. He taught me how to catch my first fish. And, when I fell and scraped my knee, he showed so much concern, holding my hand while dabbing the wound with a cotton ball soaked in peroxide. These were all simple little things, but I really held them in my heart. He made me feel so special, and so loved. I loved him so much, and trusted him completely.

When I went to bed that night on the camping trip, I would never in a million years have thought that I'd wake up to him spooning me in my tent. I can't believe what was going on, so I lay there, paralyzed, while his hands explored my body, touching me in places I'd never been touched before.

I can feel his breath on the back of my neck.

My heart shatters as I hear him fumbling with his belt.

When he gets it undone, he is much more aggressive than the man that violated me when I was eight.

All I can think is, "How can he *do* this to me? What happened to my uncle?!" I cry so hard I can't catch my breath. Where is everyone? How can nobody know that inside this tent, my world is ripping at the seams?

He whispers to me, "Want me to teach you how to make love? It feels good, doesn't it?"

To this day, this remains the most disgusting thing anyone has ever said to me.

I want to scream, but nothing comes out. All I can do is cry uncontrollably. After a constant tug-of-war as he tries to undress me and I hold onto my clothes for dear life, he gives up. I can hear him lying there, trying to catch his breath. As his breath slows, I wish it would just stop, forever.

He disappears from my side, and I'm left alone in the rest of what I remember as the coldest, darkest night of my life. Restless, lifeless, empty, enraged. The last hot tear streams down my face as I think about how to handle the situation.

I decided to share what happened only with my closest cousin. She had a close relationship with my uncle too, and I wanted to be sure what happened to me never happened to her.

When I told her, she was just as shocked as I had been, and kept shaking her head in disbelief. I felt terrible for being the person to expose my uncle for the creep he was, but I knew I had to. My cousin and I made a vow to always watch over each other when my uncle was around, so we could prevent anything like this from ever happening again.

I didn't tell anyone else, because of the thought of what this would do to my aunt. She loved my uncle so much, and if I told her, she would be so unhappy, and who knows what else would happen. Maybe they would get a divorce, and it would all be because of me. I loved her more than I hated him. Letting the truth out will only cause more harm than good, I thought — not just to my aunt, but to many of my loved ones. So, I put it out of my mind.

Three years later, I'd just graduated high school and started working for an internet company called Clearwire. This company had kiosks instead of Best Buys — I was a floater who worked in both the Nimitz and in the Aiea stores. As a kiosk worker, we were supposed to help both Clearwire and Best Buy customers. The understanding was that if we helped out Best Buy's employees, they would send customers to us. Since the job was set up to where I got a commission on top of my hourly salary (and bonuses for meeting monthly quotas), I was all for this.

In between helping customers, I'd chat and joke around with the Best Buy employees, but it was all very casual. After all, I'd only been in the stores for about a month.

One day, a customer asked me if I could help them find an HDMI cord. I couldn't find it, so I asked a Best Buy employee I was familiar with. We'd exchanged small talk a couple of times, but I didn't really know anything about him other than basic work stuff. He was one of the quieter employees anyway, and mostly kept to himself. He offered to check in the back, and asked me if I want to come with him so he can show me where they kept the extra inventory, in the back of the warehouse, so next time I'd be able to find the cord myself. I gladly agreed, and followed him.

As I follow him into the warehouse, I find myself surprised by how big it is. I would've never thought that the back of the store was just as big as the front, customer-facing side. I observe as the employee scans the area in a way which makes me wonder if he actually knows where the HDMI cords are kept. I sure wouldn't — anybody would find it easy to get lost in the shelves and rows of disorganized boxes and electronic devices. It seems as if they unload shipments wherever they find space for the boxes to fit.

I pass by DVDs, refrigerators, and car stereo systems scattered about. We head down one row, and another, and another. He's quiet. He glances back and gives me a dry smile, which makes things a bit awkward. Maybe he just doesn't know what he's doing, I think to myself.

We reach the very back of the warehouse, where it is totally isolated. He glances around, and as I follow his line of sight. I realize that there's no one around.

He gestures toward an empty shelf and says apologetically, "I guess we're all out."

I start to feel annoyed. This was such a waste of time. I think of the customer, who's been waiting on the floor for at least ten minutes by now and start to make my way back. As I thank him for taking the time to help me and head back to the store floor, he grabs my wrists and pins me against a shelf.

I pull my wrists free and beg him to stop.

He forces himself on me and starts kissing me instead.

I knee him in the groin, and he folds at the waist.

What was he thinking?! And how could I have been so clueless? I'm beyond baffled trying to wrap my head around it all. I turn and run back to the floor as tears well up in my eyes.

This time, I finally gathered the courage to say what had happened. And where did that get me? To a seat in the store manager's office, telling my story through tears while the store manager questions my motive. I was so offended, and so embarrassed for coming forward.

He kept asking me why his employee would do such a thing. "He is married with kids! Are you sure you really want to move forward with this accusation?'

he says. Tears of pure anger burn down my face as I sit there as I'm being told that I'm getting sent home to clear my mind.

When my boss at Clearwire found out what had happened, he immediately called me to tell me he was removing me from working at that location, and assured me that there would be consequences for the man who assaulted me. He got suspended for a couple of weeks, and then came back as if nothing had happened.

I got transferred permanently to the Best Buy in Aiea, and got a new kiosk in Circuit City, too. And, for a month or so, everything was fine. My boss checked in on me often, to make sure I was OK, and he even assigned security to walk me to my car at night.

I was working at Circuit City one night when I got a text from a coworker at the Best Buy store right down the road. She told me that the guy I'd turned in for sexual assault was at the store, asking where I was. I immediately felt my stomach drop and my heart start to race. The world blurred around me as I started to hyperventilate. It was like all that existed were the thoughts in my head: "He's here. He's found me. He's here." I told my boss, who let me go home, and immediately went down to Best Buy himself. When he got there, it was too late, the man had already left the store.

I tried my best to keep my position with the company, but I couldn't shake the constant fear about this man stalking me at work. After a little while, it wasn't worth it anymore. I left.

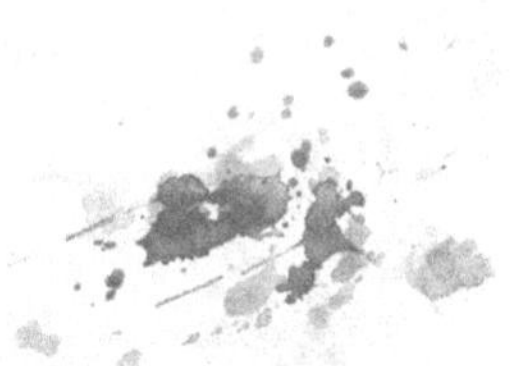

By this time, I had entirely lost my sense of peace. I constantly cried myself to sleep, letting the images of these evil men take over my mind again and again. They still had power over me, years after the actual assaults. I was sure that I was going to die alone, and unable to ever experience true love, and that broke my heart. I have always, constantly, given love to those around me, but I hardly received it in return — not in ways I wanted, anyway.

I lived like that for a long time, moving through life helpless, in a toxic bubble of distress.

Days, weeks, years went by, and I got more and more exhausted by the idea of just living in a world where these men still had power over me. And then, finally, one day, I was fed up.

Around my 24th birthday, I realized that this had to end.

Yes, these men took something away from me.

But I allowed them to *keep* taking from me.

I had the true power in this situation now, and I would no longer let these men affect how I feel. The best thing I could do for myself was to pour all my energy into things that would benefit me, strengthen me, make me happy, not bring me down.

This meant that I had to take the hard step of no longer feeling sorry for myself. I feel like I used to spend so much time excusing myself from happiness, love, and fun because of the traumatic experiences that I went through. I slowly regained some self confidence, started to take pride in who I was, and decided that I was ready to really live. That decision radiated outwards into every area of my life. I no longer live blaming this person or that person for ruining who I am, my day, or how I felt.

I have chosen to be responsible for those things, how they affect me and my feelings. And that's why I can now be thankful for what I've been through — I'm stronger because of it.

Today, I can relive these moments, and share my story, and feel no fear. Recognizing my power, and the resilience I have as a result, is something that I'm extremely proud of. No one will ever be able to take that away from me.

Tayzsia Iversen Keohokalole

is Caleb and Shiloh's mom, a wife, a sister, a daughter, a dancer, and so much more. Tayzsia is empathetic, kind, and intuitive, always seeking the beauty in every person, every situation. She is inspired by defining her own path forward and living this quote, "no one is you and that is your power."

Tayzsia grew up in Waipahu, Hawaii. She radiates creativity and has embraced her Hawaiian heritage growing up as a hula/Tahitian dancer. Dance brought she and her husband Phil, a Tahitian drummer, together. She studied makeup artistry at the Susan Page Modeling Agency and attended Leeward Community College. Tayzsia spends her days in the sunshine with her family or working with children at the Joint Base Pearl Harbor-Hickman.

"Nothing in our lives is permanent. All of it passes."

A Whole Woman

- Billie Best

When you read my obituary, the salient details of a life lived female, you'll see the usual list of factual remains — age, born here, died there, did this, and this and this, married, widowed, succeeded by nobody, thankful, thankful, yes, yes, she did good things, writer, humorist, activist, all that, blah, blah, blah — but you won't read that I was a whole woman. Most people don't even know what that means. But let me tell you, it's quite an achievement, so big and so important that it could be swept under the rug and forgotten, like a lot of other women's achievements. It's not easy being whole.

In the 1960s, when I was a young girl, 12 or 13 years old, I entered an essay contest and won. At the awards ceremony, the judge, who would have been my grandfather's age, shook my hand and said quietly, looking me squarely in the face, "I've never heard of a girl named Billie, but if I had known you were a girl, you would not be receiving this award." Yes, he was a topnotch motivational speaker, catapulting me into a lifetime of rebellion with one sentence.

In high school, my classmates elected me as their representative to a teen leadership conference, which I learned when my guidance counselor told me I wouldn't be going. He said my regrettable challenges to the school dress code — it was 1971 and girls weren't allowed to wear pants to school — was what got me into trouble. The school administration had selected another more conforming girl to attend the conference in my place. I would never have known I won that vote if he hadn't called me into his office to rub my nose in the fact that my refusal to do as I was told had cost me the opportunity to represent my peers at a leadership conference. I'm sure you see the irony of this. My election was erased, but my spirit of rebellion soared.

That's why it's not surprising to me that my obituary doesn't mention my greatest achievement. The achievements of many women who rebelled against social norms have been erased. Who remembers Grace Hopper, the first woman to win the Computer Science Man-of-the-Year Award in 1969? Or Barbara McClintock, who won the 1983 Nobel Prize for Medicine for her work in genetics? Or Rachel Carson, the marine biologist who in 1962 wrote a book about the dangers of chemical pesticides? Or Katherine Johnson, who was a human computer for NASA in the 1950s doing the math on space flight? How many fans of science fiction know the original story of Frankenstein was written in 1818 by Mary Shelley, an 18-year-old girl? In a man's world, women are remembered for being pretty, not smart. The thing is, how we look is only a part of who we are.

I was born in 1954, just 34 years after the 19th Amendment gave women in the United States the right to vote. The average cost of a new house was $10,000. A new car cost about $1700. Gasoline was 25 cents a gallon, and Elvis Presley was the next big thing. It's just a list of factoids, but you get the idea. Dinosaurs roamed the Earth. Men weren't used to treating women as equals, and many women weren't comfortable being equal to men. So, for decades after 1920, most womenstill didn't vote, even though they could. In their very gendered world, men were the decision makers and women were the baby makers. Gender was destiny. Even though gender is only a part of who we are.

My own future was all mapped out for me the day I was born — marriage, kids, church suppers, and Jell-O salad as far as the eye could see. All around me, girls were talking about boys, planning to get one, scheming how to keep one, imagining their wedding, and picking out names for their children. Linda was the most popular name for girls and John was the most popular name for boys. The American dream was contagious and there was no known cure. Our jump rope rhyme was — First comes love, then comes marriage, then comes the wife with the baby carriage. I was married for 32 years. That's how I know that marriage is only a part of who we are.

The fact that I aced menopause is another thing that will probably not be mentioned in my obituary. But I'm sure you'll appreciate how I did it. After quite a few temper tantrums trying to get sweat stains out of silk, some chipped plaster from a wee moment of violence with a frying pan, a thousand nights of the living dead staring wide awake at my bedroom ceiling, and one big nervous breakdown when I lost my keys, I thought I must have a brain tumor, because what else could change a woman's personality like that?

I was in my late 40s when I called my grandmother to ask her about our medical history. My mom had had a full hysterectomy in 1965, so she couldn't help me. When I told Grandma I was calling about menopause, there was a long silence on the phone, like I was joking. "I really don't remember menopause," she said. She was born in 1907. I was calling in 2002. "It just wasn't that big a deal in the scheme of things," she said. "I guess I was more nocturnal." That's when I realized menopause might not be the life wrecking catastrophe it's made out to be. How could a woman forget her menopause? That would be like forgetting she had cancer. I dug deep into the library for answers. What I found was the Area 51 of women's medicine. Menopause could be alien forces sapping your hormones, rendering you emotionally unstable, mentally weak, sexless, unattractive and hysterical. Or menopause could be Mother Nature kissing off your reproductive obligations and launching you into a personal renaissance of wisdom, self-interest, and independence. Who are you going to believe?

It's not that menopause doesn't suck. It does. But it's as natural as menstruation and pregnancy. Tell me if this sounds familiar. A woman is very uncomfortable for many months, her body does strange things without warning, she is misshapen and loses her mind on occasion, followed by enormous doubts that she can really make it through the ordeal. And then finally she does, and she is a hero in her own mind because she knows the feelings she managed and understands the extremes of physical and emotional change she can endure. When it's over, she's a different person living a different life in a different body, renewed by her own spirit, transformed by her experience, and enlightened by her connection to the life force. So — pregnancy or menopause?

You see, our capacity for reproduction is just a part of who we are.

It's possible that the portrayal of menopause as a calamity is the propaganda of men who began to fear the advent of elder women in power around the same time Mary Shelley figured out how to sew a man together from abandoned body parts and make him talk. That was 200 years ago. Men were determined that women should not become professionals, magistrates, scientists or playwrights, so they spread the word that a woman without a working uterus was mentally incompetent. Yup. It's a conspiracy theory. I'll let you decide.

But remember, the changes in our bodies are just a part of who we are.

After my conversation with my grandmother, I chose not to be afraid of menopause, to tough it out, and manage it myself, without medical intervention. I started doing common sense things like backing away from the martinis, eating a mostly vegetarian diet, exercising daily, getting plenty of sleep, and minimizing my stress. Unfortunately, it's not over until the fat lady sings, and my inner fat lady is apparently napping. I had my last period about 15 years ago, but if I want to trigger a wasabi hot flash, all I have to do is chow down a bacon cheeseburger and chase it with a couple shots of bourbon. My body, my choice.

My menopause was just receding when my husband died. I was 54, and even though my grandmothers were widows for more than 20 years, I didn't see widowhood coming. I was completely unprepared for living my life alone. I had no vision for it. No plan. Most men have a shorter lifespan than most women. Most women age alone. The facts of life should be extended to include the birds, the bees and the bats, because the bats last a lot longer than the birds and the bees. If you're a woman over 40, this is your wake-up call. What will you be doing when you're 70? Don't put off thinking about it. Elderhood is coming for you, even though age is just a part of who we are.

When I became a wife, I should have expected to care for a dying husband. But I wasn't given the right dolls. A doll is a template. A Widow Doll could have taught me how to live the end of life the way Barbie taught me how to be a breeder. My Widow Doll would say "Good-bye" in 20 languages, and come with accessories like a coffin, a funeral pyre, mummy gauze, and a shark for burials at sea. If every kid played with a Widow Doll, death would be obvious. We'd spend a lot less money on healthcare, dying would be a better party, and virtual cemeteries would be the new social media. Maybe being a widow would lose its stigma. Because, you see, being a widow is part of who I am.

My husband and I had a farm and a big house in the country. But as a one-person household, I couldn't maintain the lifestyle I was accustomed to, couldn't manage the load of expenses, the burdens of homeownership, and the care and feeding of a farm. I loved the life I had, but my responsibilities were smothering me, my obligations were eating up all my time, and my brain was overpopulated with statistics like cost of living, interest rates, taxes and resale value. I had spent years decorating my house, curating my look, foraging for coolness and strutting my panache. Then I had to downsize. That's how I learned that stuff is just a part of who we are.

Getting rid of so much stuff made me feel worthless. Downsizing felt like I was throwing away my time. It slayed me to see how much of my life was invested in the acquisition of status symbols that had no status. I was a member of Hoarder Nation. Stuff comes in contact with our egos, drains our wallets, and multiplies to consume all available space. It's a communicable disease. Our hunter-gatherer selves evolved from the meadow to the mall, and now stuff has become pandemic.

As a career desk jockey, I had behaved as though the purpose of life is to get stuff, and the purpose of work is to get the money to buy stuff. I endured a lifetime of stress for the status of stuff. When I was stressed, I could reach out and touch my stuff, and it gave me comfort. My stuff was always there for me, a permanent reminder of who I was and what I had achieved. I lost a map of my achievements when I let go of my stuff. That's how I know our achievements are only a small part of who we are.

I had a dinner party for my favorite women and cleaning up afterward they discovered my dishwasher was broken. I had been living without a dishwasher for months because I just didn't have the money to replace it, and I didn't want to add to my credit card debt. That choice set off alarms among my friends. My precarious finances became public knowledge, and for my birthday they took up a collection and gave me a new dishwasher. Without my husband, my friends became my safety net. My circle of women became my significant others. They cared for me and saw me through the most difficult time in my life. That's when I learned that our capacity for friendship is a very important part of who we are.

Now I live in a world without men except the few surviving husbands still in my orbit. In most of the places where women my age gather, the men have disappeared by divorce, disability, death or disinterest. In their absence we seem to recognize that the pain and sadness of losing a life partner is a passing phase. Elder women bloom in the wake of loss as they rediscover themselves, their abilities and their interests. A late life revolution in our sense of self awakens our resilient minds to new possibilities. Not that we don't love men. We do. But we learn to live without them, because being half of a couple is just a part of who we are.

These days I'm living in a studio apartment in the city. The simplicity gives me freedom and focus. I have new dreams as I age alone, living forward, hungry for new experiences. To keep from drifting into a negative state of mind, I try to practice good mental hygiene. I sit and meditate. I walk beside wild water. I will mself to stop wanting what I do not have. I seek ways of being that don't feed my anger. It takes initiative to be happy. I'm working on it.

The passage from my 40s to my 60s was a master class in change management. Everything in my life changed and, even though I felt like I was at the peak of my powers as a woman, there were times I felt out of control and out of tune with myself. Now, with perfect hindsight, I see the whole life process as the integration of my experience with the goal of achieving self-acceptance, an appreciation of myself that leads to inner harmony. How I look, my gender, my body, my age, my relationships, my attachments, my achievements and my dreams for the future — each of these is a player in the orchestration of me. I compose myself and the inner harmony I feel is wholeness.

Nothing in our lives is permanent. All of it passes. Except the voice inside. Listen. When we hear ourselves, our native intelligence shines, our common sense comes to the rescue, our intuition guides us, and our perspective becomes our strength. It is this inner connectedness of all the different parts of ourselves that develops with age to give us our power and resilience. It's taken a lifetime, but I'm finally whole. And that's how I'd like to be remembered.

Billie Best is a writer/blogger living in Portland, Oregon. Her memoir from Widowspeak Publishing in March 2020 titled "How I Made a Huge Mess of My Life (or Couples Therapy with a Dead Man)" is a provocative, at times hilarious, account of her midlife mistakes and misadventures and how they built her strength. Her blog Beyond 60 — Loving Life, Staying Relevant is posted Wednesdays at billiebest.com. Her next book will be an anthology of her most popular blog posts titled "I Could Be Wrong" in September 2020.

"I still believe politics is an honorable profession but only if we elect honorable people."

This will never be written in my obituary:

She was really short!

She cut her own hair.

When she followed her gut she made the best life decisions.

She wore the same bras for 20 years.

She never let anyone take a picture of her when she was having a "bad hair day."

She believed in God and hoped that belief was well founded.

She really didn't like the Old Testament. "God had favorites and rained down burning hail on the women and children of Jerico. Not good."

She liked beautiful table settings.

She was very comfortable with anger, both her own and others.

She inherited her Mother's love of the symphony and ballet. Her favorite was Swan Lake.

The first music she remembers was a Chopin Polonaise. Her mother played the record in her room since she was a tiny baby.

Her heart hurt because people were hungry and homeless.

She didn't like Donald Trump one little bit. Called him "crude."

She gave away a lot of money.

She could be VERY opinionated.

She excelled at public policy but was marginal as a wife and mother.

She understood power.

Her husband Bill was her rock and she was lost after he died.

I'm not who I was raised to be.

I was raised to marry, join the Junior League, raise clean, well mannered children and pretty much be at my husband's disposal for short notice dinner parties. But that's not how it turned out.

I'm a politician.

And a proud politician who served 20 years in elected office and both the state and local levels.

I got here by sheer accident. But headed in that direction, I'd never felt more at home, never had a more intuitive and instinctive understanding of what I was doing or where I was in the political universe; never had a more clear sense of direction and self.

When you feel it, go with it!

I grew up the baby of a family in Kansas where my dad made and lost fortunes in the land development and construction business. He and my mother sent me to the University of Missouri where the Fowlers had gone for generations and where, according to him, it was the best place to find a suitable husband. And I found one. I married, moved to Chicago, had a beautiful daughter and set an elegant table.

Then came the women's movement of mid and late 60s. It was stunning. My husband was a wonderful person, we had a beautiful little girl and a promising future, but the marriage could not survive the strident call to independence and self expression of the times. I was never a bra burner, but it was suddenly clear that being a home maker wasn't all there was to life. So, in 1969, I became the second woman in Illinois to divorce under the newly adopted "mental cruelty" law. There was no such thing as no-fault divorce as we have now. Prior to mental cruelty, the only grounds for divorce in Illinois had been physical cruelty or desertion.

It was a grueling time. Everyone (including me) thought I must be mentally ill. My neighbors gossiped about how my little Ann would turn out to be a juvenile delinquent and my Mother was so embarrassed she didn't even tell her friends. To make it worse, in the court process required me to be the plaintiff and my husband the "defendant." At one humiliating moment, the proceedings the judge looked down at me and said "Young woman, you're not proving your case."

But finally, in late 1969, it was over.

In the meantime, my parents had moved to Vancouver, Washington and during the summer of 1970 my little girl and I went to live with them so I could take graduate courses at the University of Portland. And that was the best move of my life!! I met Bill Morris.

From Maupin, Oregon - population 350 - Bill was fresh from the Peace Corps and had served 2 years working with youth in Columbia. I had read about the rigorous emotional and mental tests Peace Corps volunteers underwent and that only the very most stable and well balanced were accepted. So he had immediate appeal. Plus, he was darn cute. We married in December of 1970, had a son in 1972 and I loved him with all my heart until he died in January of 2018. I've not been the same since.

But back to politics – mine was a circuitous route that seemed at the time without clear ambition or purpose. But in retrospect, it was almost as straight as an arrow. And it was mostly accomplished through instinct and "connections" and that's not a derogatory term. Just as the arrow connects the bow to it's target (or not if you're a bad archer) people "connect" us from one step in our life to the next.

Until our son (also named Bill) was in the second grade, Bill and I ran a little volunteer monthly newspaper that was "down home," localized to the then "Hazel Dell" area, covered school events, had several columnists, sponsored contests like "The Plump Pumpkin," and raised money for college scholarships. We tried turning it into a commercial venture but it didn't work, and when we shut it down, I went to work as a local reporter for The Oregonian covering local and regional politics as well as the school boards and making some very special connections. In 1980 I took a position as Community Affairs Director for the newly formed Southwest Washington Hospitals but left 2 years later when Medicare cutbacks eliminated all non direct patient care positions.

Fortunately for our bank account, Congressman Don Bonker was running for re-election to the US House of Representatives and one of the "connections" I had made as a news reporter asked if I would be interested in running the Clark County part of the campaign. I said yes and from there it was almost a straight line to the state legislature. As straight as an arrow!

During my time on the Bonker campaign, I learned a whole lot about the mechanics of a campaign: signs, budgets, mailers, letters, etc. And I learned to work with people holding very different opinions. I learned there are two significant parts to a winning campaign: the hardware and the software. The hardware is all that listed above plus the more recent additions of computers, databases, social media, etc. But the software is what wins: thank you letters, remembering names, resolving disputes and all the other more tender touches. Remember the tender touches!

Don Bonker's district included Cowlitz County as well as Clark. Both were resource industry based (aluminum, timber and pulp and paper) and decidedly blue collar union. Though roughly 60% base democrat voters, the area was heavily agrarian and many of the mill workers, at least in Clark County, owned farms or timberland. As a girl from Kansas, I had a cultural respect for property rights so I fit right in.

After that November's victory, I joined Bonker's district congressional staff and headed his Vancouver office. It was a delightful time and I learned a lot about governance. Plus, I made "connections" across two counties, the counties that made up the majority of the state Legislative district I would eventually run for.

Then my time came. In 1987 Republican State House Member Linda Smith ran in a special election against then Democratic Senator Joe Tanner and won. That meant her seat in the House would be up for grabs in 1988.

When I woke up on the morning after Linda Smith's 1987 win, I knew that her House seat would be mine! I knew it as certainly as I knew my name. I knew it in my head but more importantly, in my heart and in my gut. You might call that kind of certainty arrogant and it probably was. But I'd met enough Congressmen and other elected officials that I mused "well if they can do it, I certainly can."

I ran for the seat in 1988 and won! And then another seven elections in a row, serving for the next twenty years in elected office: eight in the Washington State Legislature and 12 on the Clark County Board of Commissioners.

Remembering that I had my adult "coming out party" in the midst of the women's movement of the 60s, I've not responded to authoritarian figures very well. So Speaker of the House Joe King and I clashed on many occasions. It was just impossible for me to be obedient. But I did learn from him anyway: compromise can mean improvement in the language of public policy.

In 1994 the Democrats lost control of the House of Representatives and I was the only D re-elected from a swing district. I liked achieving goals so I didn't like the minority. Impossible to be effective! So in 1996 I was appointed in May to fill a vacancy on the Clark County Board of Commissioners and won the election that November. Bill and I were both glad there would be no more months of separation while the Legislature was in session. I liked being back home with him.

Even in this day of political rancor and disgusting discourse, I still believe politics is an honorable profession but only if we elect honorable people. Politics is the arena in which we work out our collective differences, instead of picking up guns and shooting each other. Yes, there are winner and losers, but there are winners and losers throughout nature. Good politics produces more winners than losers.

And I believe in honoring voters. They are a lot smarter and wiser than some politicians think. You shouldn't try to fool them.

Last week, I met a woman who made me wonder about the difference in how we see ourselves and how others see us. She almost embarrassed me with phrases like: "I have so much regard for you;" and "I admire all the things you've done so much." All I could think of was "Who in the world are you talking about?"

Maybe I did some good, but who knows.

I do know that I've been blessed in my life! A wonderful husband, two beautiful children and a home we built in 1978 and lived in for 42 years.

Betty Sue Morris

Born and raised in Wichita, Kansas Betty Sue Morris received her BS In Education from the University of Missouri in 1963 and her M. Ed. from the University of Portland in 1974. She married twice and had two beautiful children, a girl named Ann and a boy named Bill.

Her professional life was wide ranging from high school teacher to newspaper reporter, and eventually into elected politics serving 8 years in the Washington State House of Representatives and 12 on the Clark County Washington Board of County Commissioners.

She served on numerous civic and non-profit boards and commissions ranging from the Vancouver Symphony Orchestra Board of Directors and the Salmon Creek Legacy Hospital Foundation Board to the FISH (Friends in Service to Humanity) and FOVL (Friends of Vancouver Lake) Board.

The recipient of numerous honors and awards she was chosen as a YWCA "Woman of Achievement" in 2005; in 2006 she was named one of the "50 Most Powerful Women in Clark County" by the Columbian newspaper; and 10 years later she was chosen as a "Founding Mother" for the YWCA's portrait gallery.

In 2014 she co-chaired with former Sheriff Garry Lucas the winning "Charter Yes" campaign to adopt a new county charter.

"We are all haunted
to a degree.
When loved ones die,
their physical existence
ceases, but much of
who they were in life
remains behind."

I live in a haunted house on the Oregon coast. When my husband and I bought the 83-year-old Cape Cod last fall, we didn't know it was haunted. Maybe we didn't read the fine print close enough when we agreed to purchase the house "as is." We'd assumed that meant old furnishings and worn out tea towels. We didn't know we'd signed on to cohabitate with Maxine, the ghost of the previous owner.

Let me be clear; Max isn't your typical chain-rattling apparition. We've never seen her ghostly form roaming our hallways, and we've yet to find any ectoplasmic goo stuck to the furniture, but her essence lingers just the same. Max is entwined in the history of the house, embedded in its DNA. She's as much a part of it as the nails and foundation which support it.

We fell in love with Max's storybook cottage the minute we laid eyes on it. Perched on a bluff above the Pacific Ocean, it was our dream home. Much to our surprise, we learned that after the previous owner died, the house sat vacant for almost three years. *Why had no one bought this gem?* Sure the house needed a lot of TLC, but the bones were good, we could fix everything else.

Our friends thought we were crazy. My husband and I had both just buried our mothers after a decade of caring for them through Alzheimer's, heart, and lung disease. Over the years we'd downsized them, moved them numerous times, sat through countless doctor and ER visits, and held their hand up until their final breath. Lord knows we needed a vacation, not another project. However, we dove headfirst into the 83-year-old fixer. And our first task would be a familiar one; clearing yet another home of mementos and memories.

As we emptied the house of old furniture and personal items, we slowly pieced together a vivid picture of the previous owner. We found old photos of Max standing proudly in front of the house. Pictures of her kids and grandkids still sat on the bookshelves. As we cleaned, we learned about Max's interests; her politics, hobbies, the places she'd traveled. We discovered which books and movies were her favorites. Which recipes she liked and even her musical tastes. It's as if the house was slowly introducing us to Max, and the work became a labor of love.

Everyone in the small coastal community knew and adored Max. Every neighbor we met had a story to share about her, each more grand and exciting than the last. As Max's lore grew, we became fascinated by the Irish spitfire who had lived life to its fullest and shared that love and passion with everyone she met. In life, Max had been an outspoken community leader, a galvanizer of people, and an achiever in every sense of the word. In death, Max was nothing short of legendary.

When Max died, the community was so devastated by the loss they held a Viking funeral for her, complete with a symbolic funeral pyre. Max wasn't just a paragon of the community; she was a freaking *Viking*! Is it any wonder the community still mourns her loss three years later?

Although we've never seen Max, we feel her presence in the house. Max has been a benevolent spirit, helpful even. At Thanksgiving, when we needed a meat thermometer, a brand new one appeared in the kitchen drawer. *A gift from Max* I told my husband. And if we needed a tool, a rake or shovel one would inevitably appear — all gifts from Max.

Our first gift from Max appeared the day we moved into the house. An old CD player had been left on the kitchen counter, along with several CDs by artists we loved. We filled the house with music again and spent the day happily cleaning to songs by Etta James and Bobby Darin and Arlo Guthrie. A perfect welcome to our new home. *Thank you, Max!*

We are all haunted to a degree. When loved ones die, their physical existence ceases, but much of who they were in life remains behind. We keep their memory alive by reminiscing about them. By sharing their stories, we keep our loved ones tethered to us. We allow them to linger, like ghosts.

In Max's case, she was so beloved that the community couldn't bear to let her go. A love that fierce doesn't simply disappear; it transforms into something new.

Our family didn't buy *any* old beach house. We purchased the home of a beloved icon. The neighbors might have regarded us with suspicion as outsiders or interlopers. Instead, the town greeted us with open hearts and minds. Perhaps we've been accepted because of the good vibes associated with Max and the house. Another gift from Max.

Even in death, Max is still running the show. I'm convinced she's the reason the house sat empty for three years — Max was waiting for the right buyer. For a family who would love her little cottage and respect its rich history. A family who would embrace her community and fill her home with laughter, music, and magic once more. Max waited for *us*.

Moving in with Max has proven to be a pivotal life choice. It came at the end of a tumultuous year. The two most influential women in my life, my mother Lucille and my mother-in-law Dorothy, had died within months of each other, and my job as caregiver had come to an abrupt end.

Maybe in finding the house, I found something to care for again, something to pour my love into. And of course, I found Max. A stranger destined to become another influential woman in my life. A woman who, even in death, has shown me how to make the most out of life's transitions.

I like to imagine that somewhere in heaven Lucille, Dorothy and Max are together, kicking up their heels, sipping champagne and dancing as Frank Sinatra sings "Come Fly With Me."

When we found Max's house, we found our way home again. Of course, we know the house will never fully belong to us, we'll always share it with Max. But we're happy to do so and hope to continue her legacy of love and goodwill. I'll always be grateful to Max; she helped me find my way through the darkness and brought me back into the light of my forever home.

Thank you, Max.

Pam Grimes is an American author and humor columnist. Her first published book, *Confessions of an Edgy Suburban Mom,* is a collection of observational humor essays from her column *The Edgy Suburban Mom*. She is the 2012 Shirley You Jest! Book Awards/Shirley HAH non-fiction winner. After raising her three sons in Portland, Oregon, Pam now lives on the Oregon coast with her husband and their dog, Inca.

"Pam Grimes' "Confessions of an Edgy Suburban Mom" spins a handful of humorous yarns. The best of them, such as "The Great Toilet Paper War," sparkle to life when the author pulls back on the jokes and, with a deft, light hand, lets a great story tell itself." ~ ***Shirley You Jest! Book Awards***

"I want to have hopes and dreams and figure out how to make them come true."

My Ode to Epiphanies

- Stacey Graham

The highway between Macon, Georgia and Hilton Head South Carolina is 197.9 miles. Highway 16 is a long, desolate stretch, at least it was in 1983. There are still just 6 exits and only four have any services.

My mother and brother had flown into Atlanta from Oregon that momentous morning. Though it wasn't yet momentous, nor was there any inkling that my life was about to change. My sister was flying into Savannah, having been diverted due to something I can't now remember.

We'd been in the car for about an hour and a half and my Mom was asleep in the passenger seat and my 17-year old brother had stretched out in the back seat to catch a few winks before encountering the Atlantic Ocean for the first time.

It was Thanksgiving weekend and my entire family, now just four of us, were going to be together to celebrate. I was 30, recently divorced and had moved to Georgia with a Fortune 500 company, more than 2000 miles from family and friends. And, I digress.
I love to drive, and frankly, was glad everyone else in the car was asleep. It gave me time to think and ponder about life, my future, relaxing in a beach house and gazing out over the endless tides. Perfect.

And, then something happened. A thistle green metallic Mercedes-Benz 380SL flew by. It was the ultimate sports car convertible. I discovered them in the late 70s and had fallen in love. This was a big deal discovery because I grew up in a small town of 1,500 and I thought the only car brands were Ford and Chevrolet, as those were the two dealerships in the area. And, my Dad was a "Ford guy."

So, my very first thought as I watched this beauty pass me was "maybe if I get married again, I could afford a car like that." And my immediate follow-up thought was "and then I can go on exotic vacations again." And my third thought was, "and what if you don't get married again? Does that mean you can't have a nice car or a great vacation or a new house, or, or, or?"

And that was my epiphany. What if?

Wow. I thought of myself as an independent woman. Someone who took a leap of faith by leaving home and seeking a bigger world and new opportunities. And there I was, placing my future…my happiness in the hands of a man I didn't even know. What did that say about me? About who I really was? About who was responsible for my happiness?

So, I started thinking about what I wanted for myself and my future. Asking if I really wanted to rely on someone else to make it happen. Making their dreams mine. Or, did I want dreams of my own? Did I have the drive and desire to make them come true, whether or not I had a husband or a partner.

I said YES. Out loud. I want to forge my own path forward. I want to have hopes and dreams and figure out how to make them come true. And, if in the process I find someone to share those with, and to create additional hopes and dreams, so much the better.

That day, that moment, my life took a significant turn, even though Highway 16 is one long straight and lonely highway. I saw the possibilities.

Many weeks later, someone asked me to envision what my life would look like in five years. And in 15 years. I would describe it in living color. Where I lived. What I was doing professionally. What I looked like. I took it one step further and envisioned what I would be doing when I was 80.

I was amazed because these weren't things that I had been consciously thinking about. Yet I was. Creating a life worth living, and it all started one day driving toward the ocean.

Now, 37 years later and still not married, there are a few things I can say.

I have lived a very full and satisfying life and I am happy.

I have loved deeply and with my whole heart…. my family,

some very dear and amazing friends, some very dear and amazing men and a group of incredible kids (now adults with their own families).

I have been a leader in business, nonprofits and community organizations in every community where I chose to "hang my hat".

I have lived my life always trying to be in service to others. After all, as Ram Dass says, "We're all just walking each other home."

I have travelled across the globe which has deeply changed the way I see the world.

I have never owned a Mercedes-Benz of any kind.

As I prepare to retire and spend a year in Italy, my best advice is this: Figure out who you are and what your "WHY" is (checkout Simon Sinek's TED Talk). Then plot your path. And, always, always be open to the magic, the moment, the epiphany. I promise, it's worth it.

Stacey Graham worked for the Governor of Oregon, Georgia-Pacific, Warren Clark & Graham (advertising agency), United Way, Gard & Gerber (public affairs firm), First Independent Bank and the Humane Society for Southwest Washington. She spent 15 years in Clark County, Washington, volunteering her professional time to help local nonprofits develop strategic and marketing plans and brand strategies. She served on the Stayton Oregon city council, on many Oregon and Washington nonprofit boards and works on community initiatives in her Vancouver, WA community. She describes herself as a seeker, a wanderer, a change agent, strategist, writer, collaborator and advocate for women, children and animals.

CPSIA information can be obtained
at www.ICGtesting.com
Printed in the USA
LVHW011657110121
676201LV00024B/508/J

9 780578 751818